In his new book, "*What To Do When Your Money Is Funny*," Lee Jenkins has managed to put together a book that is entertaining, informative, biblically based, and easily applicable. Whether you are in a financial crisis or have questions about how to handle the millions you have in the bank, this book is for you. Jenkins is a financial expert whose knowledge and integrity I wholeheartedly trust. I pray that you too will be blessed by His God-given wisdom. Enjoy!

Bishop Eddie L. Long, Senior Pastor
New Birth Missionary Baptist Church, Lithonia, GA

Lee Jenkins' latest book, *What To Do When Your Money Is Funny*, is a treasure chest full of valuable financial insights from a practical and biblical perspective. It's an enjoyable, easy-to-read book that is educational yet entertaining. Regardless of where you are financially; you need to read this book—then keep it in your library as a financial reference guide.

Dr. B. Courtney McBath, Senior Pastor
Calvary Revival Church, Norfolk, VA

My good friend Lee Jenkins is an extraordinary teacher who knows how to take complicated financial issues and make them plain. He knows his God, he knows the Word, and he knows about money. That's what makes this book and his ministry so powerful!

Dr. Tony Evans, Senior Pastor
Oak Cliff Bible Fellowship, Dallas, TX
President, The Urban Alternative

Lee Jenkins' knowledge and insight regarding money is very valuable to the Kingdom of God. I have personally benefited from his ministry and expertise. If you want to be educated, encouraged, and empowered in your financial life, then this book is for you. *What To Do When Your Money Is Funny* is for those who are looking for answers to everyday financial issues. Read it and you won't be disappointed!

Teresa Hairston, Founder & Publisher
Gospel Today magazine

Lee Jenkins has delivered a truly remarkable book that I highly recommend to college students and athletes. A lot of debt and financial mishaps start in college then follow people for the rest of their lives. *What To Do When Your Money Is Funny* will help the young and the old avoid plenty of financial mistakes.

James "Mitch" Mitchell, Football Chaplain
University of Tennessee, Knoxville

Lee Jenkins has an abundance of financial wisdom. In his book *What To Do When Your Money Is Funny,* he provides life-changing solutions and practical antidotes to help you become a better steward over God's resources. This book has changed my financial destiny, and it will change yours too!

Robert Watkins, President
Kings & Priests International, Atlanta, GA

LEE JENKINS

foreword by Howard Dayton

What To Do When Your

MONEY is

FUNNY

Real Solutions to Financial Challenges

MOODY PUBLISHERS

CHICAGO

All Scripture quotations, unless otherwise indicated, are taken from the *New American Standard Bible*®, Copyright ©1960, 1962, 1963, 1968, 1971, 1972, 1973, 1975, 1977, 1995 by The Lockman Foundation. Used by permission. (www.Lockman.org)

Scripture quotations marked NLT are taken from the *Holy Bible, New Living Translation,* copyright © 1996. Used by permission of Tyndale House Publishers, Inc., Wheaton IL 60189, U.S.A. All rights reserved.

Scripture quotations marked GNT are taken from *Good News Bible,* Today's English Version. Copyright © 1992 by Thomas Nelson. Used by permission.

Scripture quotations marked NIV are taken from the *Holy Bible, New International Version*®. NIV®. Copyright © 1973, 1978, 1984 by International Bible Society. Used by permission of Zondervan. All rights reserved.

Scripture quotations marked ESV are taken from *The Holy Bible, English Standard Version.* Copyright © 2000, 2001 by Crossway Bibles, a division of Good News Publishers. Used by permission. All rights reserved.

Scripture quotations marked NKJV are taken from the *New King James Version.* Copyright © 1982 by Thomas Nelson, Inc. Used by permission. All rights reserved.

Scriptures quotations marked NCV are from the *Holy Bible, New Century Version,* copyright © 1987, 1988, 1991 by Word Publishing, Nashville, TN 37214. Used by permission.

Cover Design: Trevell Southall Design
Cover Image: Drexina Nelson
Interior Design: Ragont Design
Editor: Tara Coyt

Library of Congress Cataloging-in-Publication Data

Jenkins, Lee, 1961-
    What to do when your money is funny / by Lee Jenkins.
        p. cm.
    ISBN-13: 978-0-8024-8801-5
    ISBN-10: 0-8024-8801-3
    1. Finance, Personal. I. Title.
    HG179.J3682 2007
    332.024--dc22

                                    2007024297

1 3 5 7 9 10 8 6 4 2

Printed in the United States of America

To those who inspired me to dedicate my life

to teaching people God's financial principles:

Ronald Blue,

Howard Dayton,

and the late Larry Burkett

Thank you for your friendship, mentorship, and ministry.

CONTENTS

FOREWORD

I have known Lee Jenkins for almost twenty years, and he is an extraordinary person by any measure. Lee has been a successful athlete, businessman, and financial advisor. Even more important, he and his wife, Martica, have a great marriage and have done a dynamite job of raising mature children.

Lee's passion is to teach people how to handle money God's way, and he has effectively and powerfully done this in this book. *What To Do When Your Money Is Funny* might strike you as an unusual title for such a serious issue that holds so many people in bondage. But it is the perfect description of the condition of so many of our finances. The dictionary defines "funny" as "foolish, ludicrous, irrational, careless, or impulsive."

What To Do When Your Money Is Funny is also the perfect description of the author, Lee Jenkins. He is a gifted communicator who will make you laugh as shares his own financial experiences with transparency. The book is easy to read and contains an incredible amount of truth that will set you free—financially free. It is destined to help tens of thousands of people—and I pray that you will be one of them.

Lee Jenkins has been living the principles you will learn. They work. Lee is living proof of that—and you can be as well!

HOWARD DAYTON
Cofounder, Crown Financial Ministries

ACKNOWLEDGMENTS

First, I'd like to thank my wife, Martica, my daughter Kristin, and my sons, Martin and Ryan. Thank you all for giving me the support to carry out God's call on my life. Next, a huge thank you to my wonderful editor, Tara Coyt, for all your hard work and dedication. You are great! Also, a special thanks to Lee McCutchan for all of your wise counsel.

Another big thank you goes to Cynthia Ballenger at Moody Publishers/Lift Every Voice. I am so grateful for your assistance and encouragement.

Finally, to all the pastors and churches that have supported my financial teaching ministry; it is indeed an honor to serve you.

INTRODUCTION

HOW DID I GET INTO THIS MESS?

The fact that you have this book in your hands means that either you or someone you know is experiencing a financial challenge. It doesn't have to be something catastrophic, just something bad enough to make you worry, keep you up at night, shatter your confidence, or even worse, make you doubt whether God is going to come through for you. God didn't create your financial problems, so instead of doubting Him, I urge you to rely on His Word to resolve your problems.

If you are experiencing some tough financial times right now, I know how you feel. I've been there and I know it stinks. Like me, you probably thought it would never happen to you. Financial problems can steal your joy, wound your self-esteem, stifle your creativity, and stress you out to the max.

My guess is that you want to keep your financial problems a secret, for fear your friends, family or coworkers will think less of you. I know for sure that you want out of this bad situation right now!

NO MORE FINANCIAL DRAMA

Keep reading and you'll find out how to avoid or break free from just about any financial drama you're experiencing.

You're saddled with credit card debt. When you were in college a solicitor offered you a free mug, a T-shirt, and a credit card. You took them all, then lost the mug, wore out the T-shirt, and overused the credit card. Or maybe you signed up for a credit card after receiving a solicitation in the mail. Whatever the case, you're now in credit card debt up to your eyeballs! At first you intended to use the card only as a convenience; now you use it all the time—for shopping, to pay bills, for cash advances, and as an emergency fund when you run out of cash. You can't afford to pay the balance off every month so you barely make the minimum payment and the balance doesn't seem to be going down. What started out as a mere convenience has now become a necessity, or should I say, a harmful addiction.

Your credit score is really messed up. Years ago you had a decent credit score, but things happened—a lost job, a late payment here or there, missed car notes, maxed out credit cards, charge-offs, misunderstandings, and disputes with creditors, etc. Now your credit is "tore up from the floor up!"

The month is longer than your money. Like 70 percent of Americans, you live from paycheck to paycheck. You juggle expenses so well you could be in the circus! God forbid if you missed a paycheck. At night you're on your knees praying for just one month where you have some financial wiggle room, some peace of mind, and a surplus of funds. Perhaps you are living above your means or spending more than you can really afford. Whatever the problem, you just know your cash flow is not flowing!

You just can't seem to find a way to save money. Every time you put a little cash away, something happens; the transmission goes out, you get hit with an unreimbursed medical expense, or the kids need money, again. You've tried to save some money for a rainy day, but it seems like the rain falls every week and it's always a downpour. Without a savings account your credit card has now become your emergency fund and a way to pay for essentials, which only drives you deeper in debt.

The car you bought or leased is driving you to the poorhouse! You love everything about it—the color, the rims, the smooth ride—but you hate the monthly payments! You've even thought about returning it to the dealership, but you can't because you're upside down, owing more on the car than it's worth. Everyone who sees you driving this car thinks you're rolling in the dough— if only they knew the real deal!

You're hiding financial problems from your future spouse. Somehow you've managed to keep your financial troubles a secret because you don't want the love of your life to think you are a financial deadbeat. So you hide all the debt, the bills, the charge-offs, and the low credit score, not realizing you are planting seeds for marital discourse. No wonder 50 percent of marriages end up in divorce; we're not telling the truth about money.

You and your spouse never agree on how to allocate funds. Different priorities, family history, and culture are preventing the two of you from getting on the same page financially. You are financial opposites so you've decided to play the "my money, your money" game, making sure the finances are kept separately. Fights about money are frequent and it's affecting your sex life. Now you're living like roommates instead of husband and wife, all because of money.

You're a single parent and there never seems to be enough money to take care of the kids, the bills, and you. Pulling the financial load all by yourself is kickin' your behind and there's no one to depend on, except God. To make matters worse, the kids always need money for something and everything costs so much (food, school, clothes, activities). You're doing the best you can, but you often wonder how you are going to make it.

Your dream house has turned into a nightmare. You *had* to have this house, so you took out one of those "funny mortgages," bought lots of nice furniture, and impressed all your friends. Everything was cool until interest rates started climbing. Now your monthly mortgage payment is way beyond what you can afford (something the mortgage people failed to warn you about). A couple of homes in the neighborhood have been foreclosed and you pray your home won't be next.

Maybe you've been victimized by downsizing or got laid off. It caught you totally off guard and you found out the hard way that there was no such thing as "job security." You gave your all for your employer and what did you get for it? A pink slip! Now what are you going to do? You need to hurry up and find work. You don't want to take just any kind of job, but you may have to. Money is getting tight.

The business you started didn't take off like you thought it would. You were going to make some big money and live large! Now, instead of becoming the next Donald Trump, you're starting to feel like Donald Duck! You dipped into your home equity, maxed out your credit cards, and borrowed from friends and relatives to get the business up and running. You still can't quite figure out what went wrong; you don't have a business anymore and you are left with the debts and the scars of a failed business.

Acquiring and managing money has always been a problem. You seem to be chronically broke, always struggling. Maybe it's a generational thing; it seems that people in your family are always a day late and a dollar short, but you are tired of it and want a better life for yourself.

Tithing never seems to fit into your budget, but not for a lack of trying. You love the Lord and want to honor God with your money, but how can you give when you have so many bills to pay? When the collection plate is passed at church, you quickly give it to the person sitting next to you, feeling guilty that you can't contribute. What are you supposed to do? Your heart says, *Yes, go ahead and give*, but your head says, *Don't be stupid. You can't afford it.*

The above list may seem long, but these are just a few real-life financial situations that millions of people go through every single day. Don't believe the Enemy who wants you to feel like you're the only person in the world going through tough money problems. As you can see from some of the above scenarios, that's a flat-out lie. *USA Today* recently reported that half of all Americans are experiencing a financial crisis of some sort. That's a lot of people! You see, you are not alone. Now is the time to turn to God who said He would never leave or forsake you.

Look here, if you are in a season in your life where your money is funny, be encouraged because the book you're holding right now will give you the support, advice, and knowledge to change your situation. God says in Jeremiah 29:11 (GNT) that, "I alone know the plans I have for you, plans to bring you prosperity and not disaster; plans to bring about the future you hope for." Can I get an Amen?

Know that God has a plan for you and it doesn't include being broke, busted, and disgusted. He wants to prosper you and give you the future you desire! Now that's good news. Just like a bad thunderstorm that passes through the night, the financial hurricane you are facing right now will soon pass. Your current situation is just a temporary condition; troubles don't last always. God has a solution for any and every financial challenge you face.

GOD CAN CHANGE YOUR FINANCIAL LIFE!

God loves to demonstrate His faithfulness toward those who trust Him—just ask Job. Mr. Job was blameless and upright, and one who feared God and shunned evil (Job 1:1). He was sailing through life as the Bill Gates of his time; the world's richest man.

Job was blessed with a happy wife, a large family, thriving live-stock, land, and agricultural businesses. Things seemed to be getting better and better every day until the bottom fell out, for no explainable reason. He lost everything: home, family, health, businesses, and money. Yet God restored Job, just like He wants to restore you.

The Bible is full of miraculous stories. Remember Simon Peter in Luke 5:1–11? He had a successful fishing business; then one day he and his partners worked hard all night and caught nothing. Like salesmen who couldn't close the sale, they were preparing to leave work that day penniless, disappointed, and tired. Then Jesus came on the scene and gave Simon Peter and his partners some divinely inspired business advice. They reluctantly obeyed God's message and instantaneously went from being broke to being blessed. God wants to do the same thing for you!

Then there is the widow in 2 Kings 4:1–7. This woman's husband died and left her in a boatload of debt. She had so much debt that the creditors were threatening to seize the loan collateral—her two sons! Only a financial miracle could save her sons from slavery, so she turned to the prophet Elisha who offered sage financial advice. Once she followed the instructions of this godly messenger, God performed a financial miracle for her. Not only did she end up debt free, but she and her two sons had enough money to live on for the rest of their lives!

The same God who restored Job financially prospered the business of Simon Peter, and eradicated the widow's debt is waiting to transform your financial life. I thought you knew . . .

1. *God Owns It All.* "The earth is the LORD'S and all it contains, the world, and those who dwell in it" (Psalm 24:1).
2. *God Wants to Prosper You.* "And let them say continually, 'The LORD be magnified, who delights in the prosperity of His servant'" (Psalm 35:27).

3. *God Is Always with You During Difficult Times.* "For God has said, 'I will never leave you; I will never abandon you'" (Hebrews 13:5 GNT).

REASONS WHY YOUR MONEY MAY BE FUNNY

It goes without saying that many of the difficult financial circumstances we face are a result of our own doing. Sometimes we make bad financial decisions, purchasing things on impulse, buying stuff we can't afford, failing to save money, or refusing to seek wise counsel. However, financial woes aren't always our fault. Every now and then something unexpected pulls the rug out from under us. As a child of God it is important to understand that the Lord can use seemingly devastating circumstances for your ultimate good. The Scripture says, "And we know that God causes all things to work together for good to those who love God, to those who are called according to His purpose" (Romans 8:28).

Beyond the obvious practical explanations, your money may be funny for four primary reasons.

First, there's spiritual warfare. There are times you can do all the right things you know to do financially—budget wisely, give generously, save consistently—and things still don't work out; all hell breaks loose! At times it may seem like for every step you take forward, you take two steps backward. That's because a lot of financial adversity is the result of spiritual warfare. This is activity we can't see with our natural eyes, but it's still going on.

Now I don't want to get spooky on you, but the truth of the matter is that Satan is responsible for a lot of the resistance many Christians face in the area of finances. The last thing the Enemy wants to see in the life of a Christian is financial prosperity, especially when it is accompanied by contentment and a kingdom perspective. People who are financially free to serve Christ are a threat to the kingdom of darkness. That's why the Enemy does everything he can to discourage us financially; he wants to keep us broke and ignorant of God's financial principles.

The mistake a lot of us make is that we try to fight spiritual battles with physical weapons. That's like trying to shoot an elephant with a BB gun; it ain't gonna work! To fight spiritual battles you need spiritual weapons. Prayer, fasting, reading, and meditating on the Word of God are spiritual weapons that must be unleashed in your life if you want to reach your financial destiny. This artillery is just as important, if not more important than budgeting, saving, investing, and spending wisely. That's why Ephesians 6:12 states, "For our struggle is not against flesh and blood, but against the rulers, against the powers, against the world forces of this darkness, against the spiritual forces of wickedness in the heavenly places."

Let me be clear, when it comes to money you are fighting a spiritual battle. Satan either wants to see you broke and ineffective or he wants to see you rich and with so much money that you become arrogant, self-sufficient, and distracted from the things of God.

Second, your money may be funny because of the Lord's discipline. God may be withholding financial resources from our lives because of sin and disobedience. He knows how to get our attention and touches our wallets or purses to say *straighten up and fly right*! Believe me when I say that you can't live any kind of way and still expect God to bless you financially. God often uses difficult financial situations to get us to abandon our sin and get back on track spiritually. Hebrews 12:6 says, "For those whom the Lord loves He disciplines." It is never pleasant to be corrected and disciplined by God, but that discipline is a sign of His deep love for us.

Third, your money may be funny to accomplish the will of the Lord. Sometimes God uses our problems, setbacks, and disappointments to fulfill His ultimate plan for our lives. Quite often

God has something bigger and better for us, but we don't know it and can't see it.

As a teenager, Joseph was sold into slavery, accused of rape, and put in jail. All the while God was using Joseph's setbacks as a setup for a greater success. The evil actions of Joseph's brothers were used to fulfill God's ultimate plan, which was to preserve their lives, save Egypt, and prepare the way for the beginning of the nation of Israel. Check out Joseph's response to his brothers, who plotted evil against him, "You intended to harm me, but God intended it all for good. He brought me to this position so I could save the lives of many people. As far as I am concerned, God turned into good what you meant for evil. He brought me to the high position I have today so I could save the lives of many people" (Genesis 50:20 NLT).

Suppose that God is using your current situation to set you up for something greater! Here you are crying over that $40,000 a year job you lost, while God is trying to get you in position to earn hundreds of thousands of dollars a year! Consider that your disappointments are simply God's appointments.

Fourth, perhaps your money is funny to develop your character. Paul told Roman believers, "We also exult in our tribulations, knowing that tribulations bring about perseverance; and perseverance, proven character" (Romans 5:3–4). Nobody likes to go through tough financial times, however sometimes our character can only be developed in the midst of trying times. The problems that we face will develop our perseverance, which in turn will strengthen our character, deepen our trust in God, and give us greater confidence regarding our financial future.

It's refreshing to know that God is in complete control of every financial situation that you will ever face. No matter how funny your money is right now, rest assured that God is in control and intends to use everything you're going through for His good purpose.

WHY A BOOK LIKE THIS?

I wrote this book because I discovered that most people don't know a lot about how to successfully manage money. We weren't taught about it at home, in school, or at church (even though the Bible contains more than 2,350 verses on money!). As I travel the country teaching God's financial principles at churches and conferences, I am constantly amazed at the number of people with financial questions. The majority of the questions I get asked are simple, common, everyday issues that people like you and I encounter; only a few of them are about complicated financial issues. This book is simply my humble attempt to deliver some of the answers you need.

I know firsthand that a lot of people are hurting financially. At some of my seminars I am often led to pray for those who are experiencing financial difficulty. I typically ask those who are struggling to stand up or come forward and then offer them a prayer of encouragement. Regardless of the size, racial mix, denomination, or economic status of my audience, every time I make this appeal at least half of the audience stands up for prayer! Sometimes there are hundreds of people standing and sometimes there are thousands. Many are crying out to God for help and some need a financial miracle, like yesterday! I suspect they are like you, needing money, hope, encouragement, wisdom, and instruction. They, like you, need to know what to do when their *Money is Funny*. The problem isn't a lack of money; it's a lack of knowledge. Hosea 4:6 says, "My people perish for lack of knowledge."

Let me tell you up front that this is not your typical financial book. You may not get goose bumps when you read it, but that's okay as long as you get answers. There is, however, a good chance that you'll have an instant desire to share this book with your friends and family.

Money is Funny is written as a lifetime resource, rather than something you pick up, read, and then forget. This book will sharpen your overall knowledge about finances, regardless of your current financial condition. It's a "must-have" resource for your personal library, sort of like a dictionary, thesaurus, encyclopedia, or cookbook. Nobody gets that excited about buying a dictionary, but they do it knowing it contains the answers they're looking for, just like this book.

Even if you are on "easy street" financially, this book will help you. If you already have your financial act together, then use *Money is Funny* to empower someone you love. Use it as a resource to guide you in counseling others. The next time your cousin Willie calls you for advice (and to borrow money), you'll be able to share something with him, other than your cash!

NAVIGATING THROUGH THIS BOOK

The book is a compilation of financial questions that my live audiences have asked over the past six years. It doesn't cover every financial situation that exists just enough to relieve some stress and stave off a few gray hairs! What I strive to do is provide vital information to solve your problems or at the very least provide the foundation for your financial solvency.

To make it easy for you, I've divided this financial resource into twelve sections (an introduction and eleven chapters) that address the main topics with which most people need help. At the start of each chapter, you will find a list of issues—Money Challenges—that are likely bothering you, and the pages where you can find the solutions. All you need to do is head over to the section you are interested in, find the topic you need, and then flip to the right page. But before you do that, don't skip "The Real Deal" that launches each section; it's my chance to share some basic biblical and practical information you'll need in order to make the smartest financial moves. The next section of each chapter is "Challenges and Solutions," which is a compilation of financial situations posed as questions. For example, a question may read, "I cosigned for a friend. How do I get out of it?" The solution (or answer) to the question contains biblical insights and practical tips on how to solve your specific financial issue. The "Ten Commandments" at the end of each chapter is a recap of that chapter's most important dos and don'ts.

Lastly, you'll find a specific prayer regarding your financial situation. For those using the book to counsel others, you can recite this prayer for the people you are helping. Prayer changes circumstances, but most of all it changes us.

Well, get ready, because your financial life is about to change! Not just because I said so but because you have embarked on a journey that will teach you how to infuse God's Word into your current financial situation. Your money won't be funny for long—this book contains all the information you need to be more than a conqueror!

You definitely have what it takes to reach your financial destiny and to live a fulfilling life. You just need a little direction and clarity, both of which are contained in this book.

CHAPTER ONE

BUDGETING AND SPENDING

THE REAL DEAL ABOUT BUDGETING AND SPENDING

They say that money talks; when it does, it usually says, "good-bye!" If you don't direct your money and tell it where to go, then believe me, it will find a way to leave you faster than a bank robber fleeing the police.

One of the smartest ways to gain control of your money is by developing a spending plan, more commonly referred to as a budget. Now don't get freaked out on the word *budget*! By the end of this chapter, I bet you'll run toward it, not away from it. Establishing a budget just means you've decided to tell your money where to go, directing it with purpose and intent. A budget is simply a plan for your spending, which allows you to manage your money in order to reach your financial goals. A budget brings order to your financial life.

Believe it or not, we all have a budget of one kind or another. For some people, it means they spend aimlessly until all the money for that month is gone. The result, in most cases, is more month than money. (How many times have you been there?) This type of "budgeter" spends all the cash they've earned and must then rely on credit cards or loans to fund monthly deficits. Then there are those who make enough money to be careless without detrimental results. The careless budgeters make pretty good money, but overspend, buying expensive indulgences on impulse because they know they can get away with it. Their money motto is, "I've got it, so why not spend it all." These spenders usually wonder, "Where did all of my money go?"

The final type of budgeters are those who plan their spending not just in their head but on paper. They don't "wing it" every month and hope for the best. These true budgeters are able to maximize their financial potential because they have a plan.

The goal for everyone, regardless of their income level, should be to become good stewards of God's resources. To do this, you must live by a plan in order to maximize your earnings and spend your money wisely, as God advises. You can't do that without living by a real budget!

According to one study by the Internal Revenue Service (IRS), the number one reason people failed financially is the inability to delay gratification. We want what we want and we want it now! That's why in order to make a budget work you must have self-control. This is a spiritual issue because it requires discipline and control of your desires and impulses. King Solomon accurately described the person who lacked self-control, "A man without self-control is like a city broken into and left without walls" (Proverbs 25:28 ESV). In ancient days, a city without walls was subject to any intruder who passed by and was thus in a state of disarray. Have you ever opened your wallet or stopped at the ATM and felt like your account had been pillaged? Without a budget, your financial "city" is prey to any indulgence, get-rich-quick scheme, or predator you encounter.

Regardless of your current budgeting style, sip on this advice:

- Budgeting is like getting in shape physically—it's a little uncomfortable at first, and it takes time, but don't give up. It typically takes three months to see the results of your budgeting discipline.

- A budget without a goal is drudgery. Don't focus on what you are giving up or can't do. Focus on what the discipline of a budget now will allow you to do in the future (save more money, get out of debt, buy a car, purchase a house, or fund your child's college education).

- Don't keep the budget in your head. Write it down on paper or use a computer software program. It's not a real budget unless it's documented.

- If married, both spouses need to do their budget together.

- Get the entire family involved in the process (that includes the kids). Budgeting is a group effort that works best when everyone is involved.

CHALLENGES AND SOLUTIONS

Challenge

What can I do to help myself get started on a budget and stick with it? I'm having trouble sticking to a budget; it just doesn't ever seem to ever work for me.

Solution

Budgeting is simple, but I never said it was easy! The reason most people's budgets don't work is because they continue to spend more than they make. No budget can fix that. Again, you may have to make some drastic adjustments to your lifestyle to get your budget balanced. There are a lot of reasons that budgets don't work.

First of all, go through each budget category shown in the "Percentage Guidelines" table (See "Helpful Tools," page 225) and compare it to your own spending. If your percentages are way out of whack, you will need to make some tough decisions. Also, make sure that you are using a system that is best suited for you. Some people use the envelope system (putting money for each category in separate envelopes), some write everything down in a notebook, others like to monitor everything by computer. Find what works for you and stick with it.

Secondly, make sure you are being realistic when establishing a budget. Many of the people I speak to and counsel get discouraged because they haven't been able to make a budgeting system work. I've found that in most cases it's because they are not being realistic. Allocating zero dollars to budget items like entertainment, recreation, clothing, miscellaneous, or some other category is unrealistic. Having a budget doesn't mean you'll never go to a movie or restaurant. So be real with yourself and then do your best to stay within those parameters. Use the "Estimated Budget" form in the Helpful Tools section to specify amounts that are realistic. Create a plan; then be sure to stick with it.

Thirdly, stay away from *people*, *places*, and *things* that tempt you to spend. (Most of the time, it's our actions that cause the budget not to work.) Solomon says, "The wise are cautious and avoid danger; fools plunge ahead with reckless confidence" (Proverbs 14:16 NLT).

Sometimes *people* in your life can trigger excessive spending and bust your budget. I remember when I was in my twenties and quite a few of my friends were professional football players. When we were together they loved to go out and eat at nice restaurants. They could afford to do it, but I couldn't! I had to let them know that I was on a budget and I couldn't afford to do fine dining every time we ate out. When you're on a budget, you can't afford to keep up with the Joneses.

Also, pay attention to *places* that prompt unnecessary spending. Malls, jewelry stores, and department stores are common budget busters. (Home Depot is my weakness!) To stick by your budget, you've got to know your weaknesses and drive right past them.

Things can also activate surplus spending, like shoes, golf accessories, clothes, food, and art. If you've made it this far without those items, then you probably don't need them. Besides, no one will care how good you look when you're standing in the poorhouse.

Challenge

What can I do to balance my budget and save money? My monthly expenses are more than my monthly income. I know I'm living above my means because I constantly live from paycheck to paycheck and never seem to have any extra money.

> **MONEY FACT**
>
> If your expenses exceed your income, then your upkeep will be your downfall.
> —ANONYMOUS

Solution

There are only four things you can do: (1) reduce your expenses, (2) increase your income, (3) find new money, or (4) do a combination of all three. Let's talk about these options.

You're not alone; the average American spends $1.20 for every one dollar earned. Yes, that's right, every time you and your neighbors make a dollar, you not only spend it all but you borrow an additional twenty cents. It's impossible to save money that way.

The first order of business before you begin to cut your expenses is to find out where your money is going. This is one of the benefits of creating a budget, because it enables you to track everything you spend and get an accurate account of all your expenses.

After that, it's time to start eliminating or reducing unnecessary expenses. This may require replacing your house or car with something more affordable. Other alternatives include moving into a cheaper apartment or finding a roommate. Even modifying small expenses like dry cleaning, eating out, and going to the movies can save hundreds of dollars each month. Put a halt to weekly shopping sprees, unplanned grocery purchases, and indulgent gifts. You must also be willing to give up some of your habits like getting your hair and nails done (ladies, don't curse me), drinking gourmet coffee, and going to the car wash every week (brothers, break out the hose and do it yourself or add it to the kids' chore list). These changes may hurt, but they're absolutely necessary if you want to end the money drought.

After reducing expenses, the next thing to do is increase your income. If you can't convince your boss to give you a substantial raise, then you may need to get a part-time job, just long enough to balance your budget. If possible, check into working a few over-time hours. Don't let pride come before your fall. Be willing to do whatever it takes (legally and morally) to increase your income.

Thirdly, you need to find some new money. There may be some things that you haven't considered that can free up extra money for you on a monthly basis—and they don't involve counterfeiting or working extra jobs. Let me list a few:

- *Stop getting a tax refund.* "What you talkin' 'bout, Lee?" Why wait until April to get money you should have in your pocket all year round? If you get a sizeable tax refund, it simply means you let Uncle Sam "hold" your money without paying you interest. That doesn't make good financial sense when that money could have been in an interest-bearing account or paying off debt. If you increase your withholding allowances (consult with your tax advisor first), you may be able to bring home an extra $100 or more on a monthly basis! Of course if you do this, you'll no longer get a big, fat refund check in the mail, but you will see more money each month. (Isn't that what you want?)

- *Raise your insurance deductibles.* The higher your deductible, the lower your annual and monthly insurance premiums will be. If your deductible is $250, raise it to $500 or even $1,000. This strategy could reduce your annual premium by $100 or more. The downside is that if you happen to have an accident, you'll have to pay more to get your car fixed. On the other hand, if you never have an accident, then you've successfully put more money in your pocket.

- *Eliminate your home telephone line.* If you get good cell phone reception in your home, you probably don't need a home phone. Even if you have to boost the minutes on your cell phone plan, you could still save $30 to $50 a month.

- *Watch those ATM withdrawal fees.* If you currently incur ATM withdrawal fees of $1 to $2.50 per transaction, they can add up to hundreds of dollars each year. To avoid these unnecessary fees, limit your withdrawals and only use your bank's ATM machines.

Challenge

How do I set up a monthly budget when my income fluctuates? I work on commission and my income varies from month to month. This makes it hard for me to establish a monthly budget.

Solution

I've been working on commissions for over twenty years, so I know some of the pitfalls firsthand. Living on a budget calls for extreme discipline when your income is commission-based, but it can definitely be achieved. The trick is making your variable income appear to be steady. That means during the prosperous months when the money is rolling in, you can't treat it like a financial windfall! Plan for the future; store up and prepare for the lean months. I call this the Joseph Principle. In Genesis 41:53–56, Joseph saved during the seven years of plenty to survive during the seven years of famine. I know a lot of successful people who have a few big months and they spend money like there's no tomorrow. Then when tomorrow comes, they've got to beg, borrow, and steal in order to survive.

Here's how a budget can help you avoid this financial pitfall:

- Begin your budget by determining how much you make annually then divide that by twelve, and that becomes your monthly income. (Don't use wishful thinking; be realistic. Commissioned salespeople are notorious for overstating how much they think they're going to earn.)

- Set up a savings account or money market account and funnel all of your commissions into it on a monthly basis.

- List your required monthly expenses and withdraw from the savings/money market account only what you have agreed to live on for each month.

- Adhere to your budget.

- Resist the urge to make large purchases when you have a big month, unless all of your monthly expenditures, including a savings account, have been met.

Challenge

How can I learn to resist the temptation to spend? I find myself buying things I don't really need, especially when they're on sale!

Solution

Stop buying on impulse. The next time you are at the mall or your favorite store and you get the urge to spend, just don't do it! Instead, go home and ask the Lord whether you should make the purchase. Then take forty-eight hours to think about it. I guarantee you, after forty-eight hours the urge to buy whatever you wanted to buy will go away half of the time or you'll realize there's a bill that needs to be paid!

Spending money on impulse is a difficult habit to break for those who have money and is detrimental for those who don't. If you are spending so much that it's affecting your finances and your family, then you may be a "shopaholic." Sometimes our spending habits are symptomatic of what's going on inside of us and may require counseling to resolve. I've seen people spend because they had low-self-esteem, were depressed, or wanted to be accepted by a certain crowd. Whatever the case, make sure that you deal with the "root cause" of your shopping habits.

Challenge

What's the best way for me to track my spending?
I've heard about the envelope system. Can you tell
me if it's helpful and how it works?

Solution

Yes, the envelope system is one of the best ways
to organize your finances and spend wisely. It may
not work for every category of spending you have
(since some budgeted items you'll pay by check
or with automatic withdrawals), but it works great for tracking
categories like food, clothing, gas, entertainment, and miscellaneous expenses.

Here's how it works:

> **MONEY FACT**
> At least 70 percent of Americans live from paycheck to paycheck.

- First, you must have a budget in place. Establishing a budget helps
  to create the categories needed for the envelope system and to
  determine what amounts of money should be allocated to each
  category.

- After you've categorized your cash expenses, fill each envelope
  with the money allocated for it in your budget. For example, if
  you allow $400 for food, put $400 in cash in your food envelope
  for the month.

- Once you've spent all the money in a given envelope, you're done
  spending in that category. If you go on a shopping spree and
  spend all of the $200 you had allocated for clothing, you can't
  spend anything else on clothing for the rest of the month. If, for
  some reason, you decide to spend more than what's allocated for
  a particular category, you will have to reduce the amount in another category to make up the shortfall. Perfecting the envelope
  system will take time, but let me tell you—it works!

Challenge

*What can I do to ensure that I always make the right financial
decisions?* I've made a few ill-advised financial moves and could
probably make better decisions with a little help, but I'm a very

private person when it comes to my finances and don't like for anyone to know my business.

Solution

No one makes all the right financial moves all the time. Even some of the wealthiest people I know have made some bad money decisions from time to time. That's why it helps to have a financial professional to help us make wise decisions.

Most people who make poor financial decisions do so because they did not seek wise counsel *before* making the decision that got them into trouble. Some people refuse to be swayed from decisions they've already made up their mind to pursue, while others let pride prevent them from seeking advice. As a man, I have to admit that we can be especially prideful when it comes to seeking financial counsel. We don't even ask for directions when we're lost, let alone financial counsel!

No matter how smart we think we are, everyone can use a little assistance. "Fools think their own way is right, but the wise listen to others" (Proverbs 12:15 NLT). Before making a major financial decision, you should subject it to three sources of counsel:

1. *The Word of God.* God's Word clearly provides answers to our questions and concerns regarding money.
2. *The Peace of God.* Sometimes God gives us an inner peace or an apprehension about a certain financial move. Even if you have the money to do what you want, never override the peace that God gives or the caution light He provides.
3. *The People of God.* Opening yourself to a broader perspective and alternatives you might have never considered will expand your knowledge and experience. God constantly sends people to us who can help us make better

decisions; therefore, don't hesitate to consult your financial counselor, spouse, parent, friend, or church leader, in order to achieve the goals you desire.

Challenge

Our family's income was cut in half when my husband lost his job. *We realize we have to make some changes, but where do we start?*

Solution

You are not alone; 2.4 million Americans have lost a job since 1991! It now takes longer than ever before to find a new job and even when you do, it may offer a lower salary, no health insurance, and fewer benefits. First, thank God if you find a job, even if it provides a lower income than you had before.

I personally know how it feels to have your income cut almost in half. After the September 11, 2001, terrorist attacks, the stock markets went into a drastic nosedive, and unfortunately so did my business. At the time my family and I were living in a huge mansion (our dream house) that we could easily afford. However, the temporary downturn in our income caused us to do some serious soul-searching. We became increasingly aware of how the house was consuming our future wealth and depriving us of total financial freedom. That led us to make a tough but smart decision. We decided to downsize. Now we are happier in our current home than we ever were in our so-called "dream house"!

In Joel 2:18–27, Joel delivered a message for the people of Judah: God promised to drive away the army of locusts and restore the pastures again. In fact, God said He would deliver such "bumper crops" that would more than make up for the years depleted by locusts! I believe God can do the same thing for you too! Trust that God will restore you financially!

To deal with this adverse situation and keep your finances on track, *some major adjustments are required.* In a practical sense, you are going to have to dissect every area of your finances. Start by taking a serious look at what you spend on food, clothing, automobiles, entertainment, vacations, private school, and especially the house. You may have to temporarily scale down some major expenses—sell your home and buy a smaller one or rent an apartment and replace your car with one that requires a lower monthly payment or none at all.

You should also consider a part-time job, but be careful that it doesn't add more stress to your life. A part-time job is not always the answer, especially if it jeopardizes your health, time with your family, or your relationship with God. The important thing for you right now is to be realistic, do what you have to do, trust God, and learn to be content.

Challenge

I know broke people need to budget, but what about those of us who are living well and who don't need to watch every penny?

Solution

It doesn't matter how much money you earn or have saved, everyone can benefit from a budget. I'm sure you've read the stories about such celebrities as M. C. Hammer, TLC, and Mike Tyson, to name a few. They were all very high income earners (Mike Tyson earned over $300 million during his career), yet ended up broke or close to it! If it happened to these millionaires, it can happen to anyone.

Proverbs says, "Look after your sheep and cattle as carefully as you can, because wealth is not permanent. Not even nations last forever" (Proverbs 27:23–24 GNT). This Scripture is a reminder that regardless of your wealth, it is necessary to carefully monitor your riches because there is no guarantee they will last forever.

Challenge

When money is tight, which bills should take priority over others? I simply don't have the money to pay all my bills some months, but I still want to be responsible with the money I do have.

Solution:

When money is "too tight to mention," you need to prioritize your bill paying based on what's best for you and what will cause the fewest and least severe repercussions. Just because a certain creditor barks the loudest doesn't mean they should get paid first, second, or even third for that matter. When you can't pay all of your bills in a timely manner, follow these rules:

- *Necessities are first.* These are things that you absolutely need in order to live, in this order: You need a roof over your head, so pay the rent or mortgage first. Then you need to be warm in the winter and cool in the summer, so pay the utility bills. In most cases, transportation is vital, so pay your car note. Men, if you've been ordered to pay child support, then pay it! Take care of your babies or you will end up in jail. Besides, your children are your responsibility and don't deserve to suffer. Also, if you are the primary breadwinner in your family, the last thing you want to do is die and leave your family penniless, so try to pay your life insurance premium; try not to let it lapse during tough times.

- *Priorities are second.* Government-related obligations, like IRS taxes and school loans, should be paid timely. Instead of avoiding these responsibilities, communicate with such agencies and they are likely to cut you some slack.

- *Everything else is third.* Items that are not necessities, such as credit cards, department store debts, and payments for furniture and appliances, have to be put on hold until you are able to pay them timely. This doesn't mean you should completely avoid these creditors. Contact each of them and try to arrange smaller payments or deferments.

Now let me tell you what's going to happen with these bills for "everything else." Once you fall behind on your payments, the creditors will call. Then you'll start getting letters demanding payment. If you know your situation is short-term, try to explain it to them and they may negotiate better terms for you. If your situation is more long-term, then you might as well ride it out. The creditors will turn your bills over to collection agencies. Now this is not the best scenario in the world, but it's not the worst either. You've actually protected yourself. Why do I say that? Because other than damaging your credit score, there's very little these lenders can do to you. If there's no collateral behind the money you owe them, there's nothing they can take from you. They made a bet on you and they lost (creditors know they'll lose a certain amount of money on clients who can't pay). I'm not suggesting that you avoid your responsibilities, but if your current situation prevents you from temporarily paying bills, there's nothing you can do about it.

Challenge

Does God really care how we spend our money? I give my tithes (10 percent of my income) to the church; therefore I think I should be able to do what I want to with the other 90 percent.

Solution

God is deeply concerned about how we spend our money. As a matter of fact, every spending decision we make is a spiritual decision! Handling money is a spiritual issue. Why is that? It's because everything we have belongs to God! It is His money, every bit of it, not just the 10 percent tithe but the whole thing! Psalm 24:1 says, "The world and all that is in it belong to the LORD; the earth and all who live on it are his" (GNT). Since God owns it all, that makes us stewards, and as stewards of God's wealth, we have a responsibility to be faithful with His money.

Every time you go shopping or play the lottery (yes, some of the saints do gamble), you're spending God's money. One day we all will have to give an account to God for our time, talents, and treasures (money). I don't know about you, but I want to hear the Lord say, "Well done good and faithful servant . . . enter into the joy of your master!"

TEN COMMANDMENTS FOR BUDGETING AND SPENDING

1. Thou shall not "wing it" with thy finances. (Thou shall always live by a budget.)

2. Thou shall not spend more than thou makes.

3. Thou shall not try to keep up with the Joneses. (They're broke too.)

4. Thou shall always get godly counsel regarding major financial decisions.

5. Thou shall not buy on impulse. (Remember the forty-eight-hour waiting period.)

6. Thou shall practice delayed gratification. (You don't have to have everything now.)

7. Thou shall balance thy budget, even if it means reducing thy lifestyle.

8. Thou shall stay away from the people, places, and things that cause overspending.

9. Thou shall use the envelope system or some other system to track spending.

10. Thou shall learn to be content with what thou hast (whether much or little).

PRAYER

Dear Lord, I acknowledge that everything in the heavens and the earth belong to You. I am a steward and You are the owner of all that I possess. Help me to be faithful with all of the resources You have placed under my care, no matter how great or small. Help me to be disciplined and more strategic with my spending. Help me to learn how to be content. Give me insight and wisdom on how I can cut unnecessary expenses out of my life. Lord, I also pray for increase and opportunity. Enlarge my territory so that I can earn the income I am capable of earning. I realize I can do nothing without You, so I ask for Your help today, Lord. Help me learn how to live beneath my income. Help me to budget and spend wisely. I pray for financial unity within my household, and also that my spouse and I will work as a team and not as individual parts.

I recognize that it is You that gives us the power to make wealth, so that Your kingdom can be established. Therefore Lord, help me to further Your kingdom in all that I do. In Jesus' name I pray. Amen.

AUTOMOBILES

THE REAL DEAL ABOUT AUTOMOBILES

Check out my new ride! The purchase of an automobile can be one of the most frustrating or most exhilarating feelings you can experience, especially when buying a new one. There is nothing like the smell, feel, and look of a brand-new car!

Most people never forget the first car they owned, even if it was a piece of junk! For some people, a car purchase is pure emotion; practicality gets thrown out of the window! It's like when your best friend falls in love with someone whom everyone else considers to be a jerk. There's absolutely nothing you or anyone else can say to change their mind. Every automotive marketer knows that car purchases (and most other purchases) are fueled by emotion. Maybe that's why some of the craziest financial decisions I have ever seen deal with automobiles.

For some reason when it comes to cars, otherwise rational people lose their minds! Perhaps it's because many Americans have a love affair with their cars. Cars are no longer just something to get us from point A to point B; they're an extension of who we are. This is such a dangerous mind-set. If your car is seen as an extension of your personhood or value, you're in for a world of trouble, especially if it's soaking up all of your money. If you knew most people's financial situation, then took a look at what they drive, you'd interpret their vehicle as saying, "I'm insecure, gullible, stupid, young, foolish, maxed out, and broke!" even though they wanted to say, "Look at me. I'm important. I've made it."

When the average person adds up the money spent on cars in a lifetime, they'll see that it's the second largest expense they'll incur! For people who get the "car bug" every three to four years (we'll deal with this issue later), buying cars could very well be the *most* expensive purchase made over their lifetime. Imagine that —spending more on cars than on a place to live! It doesn't make sense. That's why it's important for people to learn how to make good financial decisions regarding automobiles.

Unfortunately, most people live way beyond their means when it comes to automobiles. This is especially true with men. The fascination most men have with cars probably starts during their childhoods. I can remember playing with cars as a child and imagining driving the baddest car on the block! Growing up in the black culture, a person's car was symbolic of how well he or she was doing financially. If your parents owned a Lincoln Town Car, Cadillac, or even a "deuce and a quarter" (a Buick Electra 225), then you were big time! Instead of discussing having money in the bank, real estate investments, or a stock portfolio (probably because they didn't have any), the men folk talked about their "rides."

Sadly, things haven't changed very much. It's the car that determines whether or not someone is perceived as being financially successful. That's a shame.

If you or someone you know is driving in style, but having a hard time taking care of basic necessities, consider what Proverbs

12:9 says, "Better to be a nobody and yet have a servant than pretend to be somebody and have no food" (NIV). I think the Lord is calling out a lot of people with that one. He's saying it's better to have a low profile (have money and drive an affordable car) than to pretend to be a "baller" and have nothing to eat! In other words, it's time to stop faking it! Driving a Mercedes Benz doesn't automatically make you more successful than the man or woman driving a Ford Taurus (they might be driving to a million dollar home while you head for your one-room apartment)! It's much more important to actually *be* a person of value (honoring your debts, preparing for your family's future, and saving money) than it is to *look* like you've got it goin' on.

CHALLENGES AND SOLUTIONS

Challenge

Should I lease or finance my next car? A car salesman ran the numbers and showed me that my monthly payments would be lower if I leased rather than financed my next car. It sounded like a good deal to me, especially since the payments were lower.

Solution

Trust me, leasing stinks for most people and it probably will for you too. *Consumer Reports* says that leasing a vehicle is one of the biggest consumer rip-offs. In effect, you are renting to own. Financing a car and owning it outright makes more sense than leasing.

I know, leasing a car means less money out of your pocket. How on earth can that be bad? First, let's start with why the payments are lower on a leased vehicle versus one that's financed. (You need to know this because the leasing agent or salesperson uses the lower monthly payment to seduce you into leasing a vehicle.) When you lease a car you pay only the amount the vehicle is projected to depreciate while you have it. At the end of the lease you return the car to the dealer and walk away with nothing to show for it (sort of like renting an apartment). Also, once the lease-term ends, your car will have a residual value, which is how much it's estimated to be worth at that time. For instance, if a car cost $30,000 to lease, and at the end of the lease has a residual value of $10,000, that means that it has depreciated $20,000. The money you've paid on the lease represents that $20k depreciation cost, plus finance charges and other fees.

On the other hand, when you purchase a car by financing it, you pay for the entire vehicle over a period of time. In the end, you own the car (sort of like buying a house). The fact that car purchases carry this added cost of "ownership" is what makes buying a car more expensive, on a monthly basis, than leasing it.

Below are some potential leasing pitfalls:

- Almost all auto leases—98 percent—are for new cars, which rapidly lose value. (We will deal with buying new cars versus used ones in the next question.)

- Many dealers advertise a very low payment on a car lease, which in turn requires a large down payment. The problem with this is that the large down payment is gone at the end of the lease and so is the car. This leaves you with nothing to "trade up with" for your next vehicle.

- Lease interest rates are not disclosed on the contract and very high rates can be well concealed by a greedy dealer.

- Many leases are computed on driving 12,000 or 15,000 miles per year. Most people drive way more than that! There are per-mile charges for exceeding the annual amount. If you anticipate high mileage, purchasing your car may be a better choice, since penalties for going over the limit can be very costly.

- When you lease, you never own the car. At the end of a lease, you have three choices: 1) You can buy the car outright at a prenegotiated price, which is usually higher than the actual value of the car, 2) you can walk away and look into buying another car altogether, or 3) you can simply lease another car (which is what most people do) and start the three, or four, year process all over again. If you want to have monthly car payments for the rest of your life, then go ahead and lease! To me, that just doesn't make sense.

As you can see, I am not a big fan of leasing. I just don't believe it's a good deal for most individuals, outside of a few business owners and those who are self-employed.

Challenge

Should I buy a used car or a new car? I just don't see why buying a used car is a smart move. I really want to buy a car, but why should I inherit someone else's problems? A new car comes with a great warranty. And I think I deserve a new car!

Solution

The "I deserve it mentality" has caused a lot people to make ill-advised financial decisions. I know you work hard for your money and you want to reward yourself, however, I encourage you to think about the long-term ramifications of your decisions. Timing is everything. Furthermore, just because you buy a used car doesn't necessarily mean you're inheriting someone else's problems.

> **MONEY FACT**
> One study of American millionaires found that less than 25 percent own a new car, less than 20 percent lease a car, and more than 80 percent own a two-year-old car with no payments.

There are some great used car deals out there, especially in the luxury category. I have heard almost every excuse in the book for why a person should buy a brand-new car. I even had one lady tell me that since Jesus asked for a young donkey to ride (John 12:14) that Christians should always drive cars that haven't been ridden. In other words Christians should always buy new cars. Wow, what a stretch!

To me, the new car/used car dilemma is pretty simple. Unless you are "rollin' in dough," I suggest you buy a pre-owned vehicle (that's the car dealer's way of making "used car" sound nicer). Here's why: Vehicles begin depreciating in value as soon as they leave the dealer lot. They continue to lose value each year as they are driven. A typical car will lose 30 percent of its value the first year; 17 percent more in year two; 8 percent more the third year; 6 percent more in year four; and an additional 5 percent in year five. That means the car has only 34 percent of its original value after five years. When buying a pre-owned vehicle, the original owner takes the depreciation hit, not you. Plus, you can get a great car for much less than the new price. If you want to know what used cars are selling for these days, check out the following websites: www.KBB.com, www.Edmonds.com, and www.Carmax.com.

The best deals are usually found with individuals rather than car dealerships because the individual owner is eager to get rid of their vehicles. Look in your local newspaper and find out what's for sale. The bottom line is, you always get a better deal buying used instead of new.

Challenge

How do I know if I'm getting a good deal on a new car? I've heard about all of the advantages of buying a pre-owned car; however, I still want a new car!

Solution

Be willing and prepared to negotiate. Unless the car is very popular or on back order, *there is room to negotiate the price of a vehicle*, but you have to do your homework. Here are some things to consider before purchasing a new car:

- Negotiate from the invoice price, not the manufacturer's suggested retail price (MSRP). The invoice price is what the dealer paid to get the car from the manufacturer. You'll find it on the sticker and the MSRP. The MSRP might be $25,000 but the invoice price could be $22,000.

- Find out if there are dealer incentives on the vehicle you want. These are factory-to-dealer enticements that reduce the dealer's true cost of buying the vehicle from the factory. Manufacturers offer these incentives on a regional basis to generate sales on specific models. They don't advertise these deals, so you need to do some research on your own. If you find out that a dealer incentive is being offered, you may be able to negotiate an even lower purchase price. Check out **www.carsdirect.com** or **www.edmunds.com** for information on dealer incentives.

- Don't discuss financing options or trade-ins with the salesperson until after you have agreed on the purchase price.

- Always be willing to walk away from the deal if it does not seem reasonable.

Challenge

What should I do since I want to sell my car but I'm "upside down," owing more than it's worth? I cannot afford the car payments I have anymore. I need to give the car back or just sell it; unfortunately, I just found out that I owe more than the car is worth.

> **MONEY FACT**
> People increasingly wear their cars like ID badges.

Solution

You can't just give your car back to the dealer or company that financed the car. That would be a breach of your contract. If you gave the car back, they would sell it at a discount, then sue you for the difference. Instead, try to sell the car yourself. You'll get more for it that way. Whatever you sell the car for, give the proceeds to the lender and then sign a note for the deficiency (the difference between what you sold the car for and what you owe). You'll still lose money, but it will be less than if you simply gave the car back.

Some car dealers may allow you to trade in your car and roll the negative equity into another vehicle that's substantially cheaper. You have to be careful if you do this because you're essentially adding negative equity from one car on to another car loan. However, if you get a good enough deal on the cheaper car, it may work. For instance, suppose your car is worth $16,000, but you owe $18,000. That means you're $2,000 upside down (your negative equity). If you run across a really great deal on an $8,000 car that's really worth about $10,000, you may be able to add the $2,000 negative equity from the old car to the $8,000 new loan. A dealer will only finance a deal like this if the cheaper car is actually worth about $10,000. That's why you have to get the cheaper car at a substantial discount, in order for this to work. Whatever you do, please don't take money out of your 401(k) retirement account to pay for the negative equity. If you do, you'll get hit with taxes and penalties (if you're under 59 1/2 years old) and it's just not worth it.

Challenge

Is it a smart move to get a home equity loan to buy or pay off our dream car? We have a lot of equity in our home and figured we might as well use it.

Solution

Financially speaking this is not a bad idea, but I still don't like it. Let's talk about why it might make sense, though. First of all, you can usually get a better home equity loan rate than a car loan rate. If you itemize your deductions, the home equity loan is deductible on your income tax. If you can make this work, you'll end up paying less for the automobile.

What I don't like about it is that when you borrow against your home, your payments can be extended for a longer period of time, meaning that you're paying less interest initially, but over time you may be paying more in absolute dollars. The problem is that I don't like to see people take money out of an appreciating asset (their home) and put it into a depreciating one (their car). Your home equity is a valuable asset. It's not preferable to disturb your equity, unless you're sure you can get an exceptional rate of return on another kind of investment (like a business, college education, etc.).

Challenge

I bought a car from a used car lot and it constantly needs repairs. I bought it because I needed an affordable way to get to work, now I can't afford to go to work because of the constant repair costs. What should I do?

Solution

You're driving and repairing a "lemon," so the first thing to do is check your state's Attorney General's office since each state has its own consumer protection laws for car buyers, known as "lemon laws." These laws help consumers deal with used cars that are hunks of junk. Buying a used car is a risk that can be minimized by hiring a mechanic to give the car a thorough checkup before you drive it off the lot. Be sure to use your own mechanic though, not one the used-car dealer recommends.

Challenge

I really wanted to help out a close friend, so I cosigned for his car loan. Now my so-called "friend" has defaulted on the payments. What should I do?

Solution

Welcome to the "I got burned 'cause I cosigned" club! A Federal Trade Commission study found that 50 percent of those who cosigned for bank loans ended up having to make the payments themselves. A colossal 75 percent of those who cosigned for finance company loans ended up making the payments! Your friend (or ex-friend) did what most people do—stiff the person who tried to help them.

Once you cosign for a loan, you are on the hook for everything! As a cosigner, you are considered the backup insurance policy, in case the original loanee doesn't pay. When you cosign for a car, the lender considers you the co-owner. The lender will not contact you when the loan is paid late every month, but the late monthly payments will absolutely ruin your FICO score. Because you cosigned the loan, your friend's bad history with the car will show up on your credit profile. Now lenders will look at your FICO score and determine that *you* are a bad risk. Oh, one more thing: If the car gets repossessed, it shows up on your record. The lender will contact you to pay the difference between the debt and the below-wholesale repo price they got for the car, which is called a deficit.

The Bible speaks to this issue numerous times: "Only someone with no sense would promise to be responsible for someone else's debts" (Proverbs 17:18 GNT). Also check out Proverbs 6:1–5; 11:15; 20:16; 22:26–27; 27:13.

Here's what you need to do: get the car paid off as fast as you can! You can ask your friend to help (good luck), but the bottom line is, you're going to have to reach deep in your pocket to resolve this problem.

Challenge

How do I know if I can afford the car I want? I know there's a way to calculate house payments, based on income. Isn't there something similar for cars?

Solution

How much cash you got? That's what you can afford. I know it sounds flippant, but financial expert and bestselling author Dave Ramsey says you know you can afford a certain car when you can pay cash for it! I can't argue with that. However, most people either can't or won't pay cash for their cars. The late Larry Burkett (another Christian financial expert, author, and mentor) said that you should spend no more than 15 percent of your net spendable income (that's your income after paying taxes and tithes) on your automobile. This percentage includes loan payments, insurance, maintenance, and fuel—everything that goes into buying and maintaining your vehicle.

For example, let's say your gross household income is $55,000 per year and your net spendable income (after taxes and tithes) is $38,500. Fifteen percent of $38,500 is $5,775, the amount you should spend annually on automobiles. On a monthly basis, that means you shouldn't spend more than a total of $481.25 ($5,775 divided by 12 months) on all of your rides, not just one.

TEN COMMANDMENTS FOR AUTOMOBILES

1. Thou shall not allow an automobile to determine thy self-worth.

2. Thou shall not lease a car (unless you are a business owner or self-employed).

3. Thou shall buy pre-owned cars instead of brand-new ones (unless you're rich!).

4. Thou shall do plenty of research before purchasing a new or used automobile.

5. Thou shall never pay the sticker price for an automobile. (Always negotiate.)

6. Thou shall never discuss financing options or trade-ins until the price of the automobile has been agreed upon.

7. Thou shall always be willing to walk away from a deal you don't like. (Never become emotionally attached.)

8. Thou shall not buy a car you cannot afford.

9. Thou shall pay off thy car and keep it as long as possible (until it gets old and ugly).

10. Thou shall not cosign an automobile loan for anyone.

PRAYER

Dear Lord, You said if anyone lacks wisdom, "Let him ask God," and You will give it generously. So Lord, I ask You to give me wisdom regarding my automobile(s). I pray that Your Holy Spirit will guide and lead me in any decision regarding my automobile(s). If I need to keep the one I have, then I pray that You would help me to be content with it until You bless me with something else. Help me not to be so concerned about my image but about pleasing You. Lord, if it is Your will for me to purchase a new vehicle, then I ask that You would guide and lead me to the right automobile, dealership, seller, and/or salesperson. I pray that I will walk in the Spirit and not be influenced by my emotions.

Give me the confidence, wisdom, and knowledge I need to negotiate a great deal. Help me to be bold! Give me the desires of my heart as I commit to be a blessing to others with my automobile. I ask these things in Jesus' mighty name! Amen.

CHAPTER THREE

CREDIT

THE REAL DEAL ABOUT CREDIT

Financially speaking, there are three types of people: the haves, the have-nots, and the have not paid for what they have! That last group has a lot of stuff, but they bought it all on credit!

In America, we like to buy lots of things; and so much of what we buy is financed or bought on credit. That's one of the reasons why having good credit is essential. Unless you plan on saving for everything you buy (like your grandparents did), you must establish a credit record. Like it or not, credit is a major part of your financial life and a critical key to building wealth, if it is used wisely. Your credit record can either open the door of opportunities for you or it can cause the door to be slammed in your face. It can be one of your greatest assets or your worst liability.

If I had to choose one practical issue that would have the greatest impact on turning around your financial situation, I wouldn't hesitate for a second to say it's your credit score. Even if you plan to make all your purchases with cash or with checks, you'll still need good credit. Insurance companies now check credit records before they agree to cover your car. Many employees check credit references before they hire you to see if you pay your bills on time, and to determine if you will be tempted to pilfer from the company coffers. Landlords want to know if you will be reliable with the rent, so they check your credit report. In other words, you cannot escape this aspect of life in America.

I am amazed that despite endless publicity, many people still don't understand why a credit score is important, much less how to make it better. Only one in eight people understands that a good credit score will help qualify them for better rates on mortgages, car loans, and such, according to a recent survey. A full 40 percent don't understand that something as simple as paying off a large credit card balance will help improve a credit score. A lot of people simply don't understand that they end up paying more when they have a mediocre credit score.

WHY THOSE THREE DIGITS ARE SO IMPORTANT

A credit score is a three-digit number that reflects your credit worthiness at a given point in time. This number, also known as a FICO score (FICO stands for Fair Isaac Corporation), determines the interest rate you will pay on credit cards, home mortgages, car loans, and insurance rates. It could even affect your ability to get a job! Just about every financial move you make is somehow linked to your FICO score. People with higher scores can often obtain lower and more favorable rates. Conversely, the lower your score, the higher your rate will be and the less favorable the terms will be.

SAY MY NAME, SAY MY NAME

It takes a long time to build up a good financial name, but very little time to destroy it. To a lender, a credit score says a lot about financial character. The Bible doesn't directly address credit, but it does speak to it indirectly: "A good name is to be more desired than great wealth" (Proverbs 22:1). Your credit score is like your name or financial reputation. Do you have a good name or a bad name, as it relates to your creditors? Would your creditors call you Maxed-Out Mike, Late-Payment Pam, or Bankruptcy Betty?

CHALLENGES AND SOLUTIONS

Challenge
What determines my credit score?

Solution
Your FICO score is determined by your spending and bill-paying habits, and your overall debt load. Nearly every financial decision you make is being tracked and monitored with the goal of determining your financial profile. The folks you do business with, from lenders and the phone company to credit card companies, constantly file reports on your financial activity to one of three major credit bureaus: Experian, Equifax, and TransUnion. These credit bureaus know what you have spent, what you owe, and if you tend to pay bills on time or let them slip. From all that raw data, the three credit bureaus calculate your FICO score using a formula developed by Fair Isaac. The formula has five elements, with the heaviest weighing on your payment history and amounts owed. Here is the formula:

THE FICO FORMULA
- Record of paying your bills on time 35%
- Amount of debt owed compared to your total credit limit.. 30%
- Length of credit history (the longer the better) 15%
- New accounts and recent applications for credit 10%
- Mix of credit cards and loans 10%

Challenge

How do I order my credit report and dispute any errors that I might find? I recently applied for some credit and, surprisingly, I was turned down. I'd like to find out why.

Solution

You can order one free copy of your credit report every twelve months from each of the three credit reporting agencies: Equifax, Experian, and TransUnion. You may do this either by mail, phone, or the Internet (www.annualcreditreport.com). For complete contact information for all three credit bureaus, including how to obtain credit scores and to report fraud, see "Helpful Tools," page 229. You may also obtain reports *and* credit scores at **www.myfico.com** or www.freecreditreport.com (These two Web sites provide a thirty-day free trial and then charge a monthly or annual fee.)

Now if you have errors on your credit report, you are in good company. A recent survey by the U.S. Public Interest Research Group found that 25 percent of credit reports have serious errors; 30 percent listed "old" accounts that should have been deleted; and 79 percent overall have some sort of mistake or error. You can file a dispute with the credit bureau (by mail, phone, or online), but I'll be honest with you, sometimes it can take a while to get erroneous information removed from your record.

Technically, the credit bureau has thirty days to process your challenge and get back to you with a response. If you hear back from them in thirty days and the company that charged your account says it was a legitimate charge, you must start dealing directly with that business. (See the sample dispute letter in "Helpful Tools.") By the way, a federal regulation that went into effect in December 2004 ensures that any business with which you are in a dispute over a charge must share information with you and promptly investigate the problem. Hopefully that will help you solve the problem, but it still may take a while to fix.

Challenge

What is considered a good credit score?

Solution

The average American has a credit score of 667. A score between 300 and 500 means that you are a huge financial risk and you are going to be hard-pressed to find a business that will want to work with you. Check out the following ranges to see where your score falls.

FICO RANGES:

720–850 Best

700–719

675–699

620–674

560–619

500–599 Worst

Your goal should be to have a score in the 700–850 range.

Challenge

What are some moves I can make to boost my credit score?

Solution

In order to boost your score, focus on what matters to the FICO folks. There are five things you can do to boost your score.

First, *pay your bills on time.* Remember, 35 percent of your FICO score is based on paying your bills on time. Therefore, the longer you make timely payments, the better your score will be. If you make late payments, your score will suffer. Simply make the minimum payment balance on the due date.

Second, *manage your credit utilization ratio.* Thirty percent of your score is determined by how much credit you have available and how much of that credit you're using. To boost your score, use *only* 20 percent to 50 percent of your available credit. Apply this formula:

Credit you're using ÷ credit available to you = Credit Utilization ratio

Example:

$$\frac{\$5,000}{\$10,000} = 50\%$$

Let's say you owe $3,000 on one credit card, but you have a credit limit of $5,000. On another card you owe $2,000 and have a $5,000 credit limit. That means your combined credit card debt is $5,000, but your total credit limit is $10,000. This leaves you with a debt-to-credit utilization ratio of 50 percent. Obviously, the lower the ratio, the better your credit score will be.

Third, *protect your credit history*. About 15 percent of your score is based on the length of your credit history, which is why you have to be careful about canceling credit cards. Canceling a credit card may actually mess up your FICO score, because it wipes out some important history. Now don't get me wrong, I'm not saying don't cancel your cards! If you have been struggling to get out of credit card debt and you know you'll be tempted to dig yourself back into a hole (which most people do), then by all means, cancel the cards! It would be better for you to sacrifice your score in the short term in order to create long-term financial well-being.

Fourth, *create the right mix of credit*. About 20 percent of the credit score is based on your mix of credit and how recently you have opened or inquired about opening new accounts. Even though I think this is crazy, lenders like to see a good mix of credit cards, retail cards, and installment loans, such as mortgages and car loans. To them, being in a little debt is a good thing! I must, however, warn you about applying for new debt. Any automobile or mortgage related inquiries that occur within fourteen days of each other are fine. The credit bureau counts them as one inquiry because they indicate that you're shopping for a car or a house. Multiple credit card inquiries are another story. They are generally not good because they could be a sign that you need money. Numerous inquiries can mean a loss of 50 to 100 points on your score!

Challenge

Is it true that canceling my credit cards would hurt my credit score?

Solution

You heard right—canceling a credit card can hurt your FICO score. But please don't twist my advice and use it as an excuse to keep your credit cards and drive yourself deeper into debt. Remember, I'm here to give you the facts and a few warnings about debt. Getting rid of your credit cards may affect your credit utilization ratio (reread the previous challenge and solution). If you have ten cards and each of them has a $1,000 limit, then you have $10,000 in revolving credit available to you. Now suppose you're only using five of your cards and those five cards are all maxed out. You're using half of the credit available to you, which puts your credit utilization at 50 percent.

Suppose you decide you don't need all those credit cards (which you don't) and you close the five cards you are not using. By doing this you dramatically reduce your credit *availability*. Now you've got fewer credit cards, but you're using all of your available credit.

> **MONEY FACT**
>
> Bad Credit? You are not alone. Almost one-third—30 percent—of all Americans have bad credit. That includes 27 percent of whites, 34 percent of Hispanics, and 48 percent of blacks.

$5,000 debt ÷
$5,000 available credit = 100% ratio

Thus, by getting rid of a few credit cards, you've bumped up your credit utilization ratio to 100 percent, which is not a good thing in the eyes of creditors. This 100 percent credit utilization ratio (or debt-to-credit limit ratio) could send your score down by 100 points. (Also see the warning about closing credit accounts under "protect your credit history" in the previous challenge/solution). The bottom line is this; don't cancel all of your unused credit cards. Keep the ones you've had the longest and cancel the ones you've had the shortest amount of time. But whatever you do, stop using them!

Challenge

I often sign up for department store charge cards to take advantage of those instant discounts. Is that a smart thing to do? I'm saving money on my purchase so it seems like a good deal to me.

Solution

No, it's not a wise thing to do, unless you like seeing your credit score take a hit. First of all, these cards usually start with very low credit limits. As a result, purchases will likely result in a high ratio of credit balance to credit limit (BL Ratio). Secondly, your score drops because you have opened a new line of credit and because of the department store's inquiry of your credit report. Finally, the credit scoring system looks less favorably on store charge cards (which give you limited buying potential) than it does on credit cards from major banks (which give you much broader buying potential). Again, your score can take a hit from three different directions.

Challenge

What do you think about credit repair clinics? I'm thinking about using a credit repair clinic to help me repair my bad credit and improve my score.

Solution

Be very leery of outfits that call themselves "credit repair" clinics. Most of them are rip-off clinics and are not legitimate. Contrary to its literal meaning, the common use of "credit repair" connotes improving one's credit score through the removal of negative but *accurate* data. There is no guaranteed method for removing accurate information from a credit report, whether it is positive or negative. However, promising that you can do so and charging money in advance is a violation of federal law, according to the Federal Trade Commission. If you are contemplating using one of the many credit repair clinics, start by asking if they will provide you with copies of all letters they send to credit bureaus on your behalf. Odds are they won't even answer.

Challenge

Somebody stole my identity and opened up a credit card account. What do I do and how can I keep this from happening again?

Solution

Identity (ID) theft is the fastest-growing crime in America, striking people from all walks of life. ID theft comes in a wide range of forms. In the most serious cases, thieves have bought cars and even houses by taking out loans in someone else's name. In other cases, the thief simply obtains another person's Social Security number and uses it to get a new credit card. On average, a victim of identity theft spends 175 hours restoring his or her good name by notifying credit bureaus, canceling credit cards, and negotiating with creditors.

Here are the initial steps to take if you have been a victim of identity theft. First, report the fraud and order credit reports from the three major credit bureaus: Equifax, Experian, and Trans Union. Review the credit reports for accounts you didn't open; then inform creditors of fraudulent accounts in your name. Next, file a report with your local police. (Keep a copy of the police report for your records.)

Here are some ways you can avoid being the victim of identity theft:

- Be prudent about giving out personal information to others, unless you know they can be trusted. Never give your information to strangers over the phone or Internet.
- Check your financial information regularly for unfamiliar charges.
- Request a copy of your credit report at least once a year.
- Maintain careful records of your banking and financial documents.

Challenge

Is it morally wrong for a Christian to file for bankruptcy? I'm behind on my bills and I'm starting to think filing for bankruptcy is the only way out of this mess.

Solution

If you are unable to meet your financial obligations, you should investigate a number of options before considering bankruptcy. If your income has been temporarily reduced because of illness or unemployment, consider cutting expenses, taking advantage of unemployment and public assistance, or liquidating assets. Another option is to restructure your debts. Debt restructuring involves manipulating your loan balances, interest rates, and repayment terms so you can meet your monthly expenses and still pay off your creditors in a reasonable amount of time.

You can also contact your local Consumer Credit Counseling Service (CCCS) office or other nonprofit credit counseling service. These nonprofit companies provide basically the same services as a professional credit counselor, but at little or no cost to you.

Psalm 37:21 tells us, "The wicked borrows and does not pay back." God's Word clearly says that believers should be responsible for their promises and repay what they owe. So the answer to your question is, *Yes, in most cases it is morally wrong for a Christian to file for bankruptcy.*

In my opinion, bankruptcy is permissible under few circumstances: 1) a creditor forces a person into bankruptcy, 2) counselors believe the debtor's emotional health is at stake because of an inability to cope with the pressure of unreasonable creditors, or 3) divorce, death, or a short- or long-term disability causes a person to consider bankruptcy. These are legitimate reasons, but even in some of these cases you still don't have to file. Moreover, I know quite a few people who filed for bankruptcy but never really dealt with the root cause of what got them in a financial mess and ended up back in the same situation a few years later. Issues like materialism, low self-esteem, greed, credit card abuse, and keeping up with the Joneses (envy) are common causes of bankruptcy.

Hardly a week goes by where somebody isn't telling me they filed for bankruptcy. As financial pressures mount in people's lives, they look for a fast and easy way out. For some, bankruptcy provides that release. In many instances, bankruptcy is simply a quick fix for bad habits. Sometimes good people get in over their heads so they file for bankruptcy, which liquidates the debt.

Bankruptcy is a legal proceeding that allows you to get out of excessive debt and gain a fresh new start financially. There are three common types of bankruptcy: chapter 7, chapter 11, and chapter 13. To avoid confusion, it is important to explain the purpose of each:

Chapter 7 bankruptcy allows either an individual or a business to discharge virtually all unsecured debts (i.e., debts not backed by collateral). Once a debt is discharged, the debtor has no further obligation toward that debt. The downside is that the debtor loses all property except where exempted by law. The property is sold off for cash to apply toward the petitioner's debt. Chapter 7 bankruptcy stays on your record for ten years.

Chapter 11 bankruptcy is for individuals or corporations engaged in business that need to reorganize their debts. They still intend to repay these debts and seek court protection while they negotiate a reorganization plan with creditors. This will also stay on your record for ten years.

Chapter 13 bankruptcy is designed for "wage earners" with relatively small amounts of consumer debt (as opposed to business debt). A debtor may file a chapter 13 if he/she has less than $268,250 in unsecured debt and/or less than $807,750 in secured debt. This stays on your record for seven years.

The bottom line is this: Bankruptcy is a serious matter. The creditors lose much of the money they are owed and the debtors lose some of the respect they previously had. Bankruptcies will stay on your credit report for seven to ten years; however, a person who has filed for bankruptcy can turn an otherwise negative situation into a positive one by making a commitment to repay what is legitimately owed. Once that commitment is made, the individual should look to the Lord's supernatural provision to help pay the money back.

TEN COMMANDMENTS FOR MANAGING YOUR CREDIT

1. Thou shall work diligently to get and keep thy credit score high and healthy.

2. Thou shall always pay bills on time (even if it's just the minimum payment).

3. Thou shall pay off and pay down debts (to ensure a good credit score).

4. Thou shall not cancel credit cards with long histories as a way to improve thy credit score (it may actually hurt your score).

5. Thou shall check thy credit report at least once a year.

6. Thou shall avoid credit repair clinics.

7. Thou shall not sign up for department store credit cards to get a purchase discount.

8. Thou shall use no more than 50 percent of thy credit card limit.

9. Thou shall not cosign for a loan.

10. Thou shall not file for bankruptcy.

PRAYER

Dear Lord, I want to honor You in everything I do. I ask You right now to help me to manage my credit with wisdom, understanding, and knowledge. I thank You in advance that every bill I owe, from here on out, is paid on time. Give me wisdom as I speak to my creditors concerning the fulfillment of my obligations. If there have been any misunderstandings, help me to clear them up immediately. Lord, help me to operate with patience as I endeavor to improve my name. Send information, resources, and people into my life that will help me deal with my credit issues. Lord, protect me from any fraudulent activity. Most of all Lord, help me to get out of debt! As I operate with honesty and integrity with my creditors, I pray that You will give me favor with them, and that they will show mercy when I need it.

Lord, my finances belong to You and so does my financial reputation. Help me to protect it so that Your name can be glorified in all that I do. In Your Son's holy and precious name I pray. Amen.

DEBT

THE REAL DEAL ABOUT DEBT

Slavery is alive and well! I'm talking about *green* enslaving those who are red, yellow, brown, black, and white. Today there are so many people held captive by the number one slave master of all—financial debt.

There is so much debt in this country that the average American is dishing out more than 92 percent of his/her after-tax income on debt payments. In other words, 92 cents of every dollar goes to paying off debt. That's a lot of money (in 1946 the amount was a mere 4 percent).

Let me translate this into real numbers; the average American household is carrying a total of $8,123 in debt on credit cards alone. That doesn't include what we owe on cars, boats, the home, or any other noncredit card purchases. If the average household were to make just the minimum required payment on each monthly credit card bill (which many of us do), it would take more than thirty-seven years to pay off the $8,123 debt and the actual payments would total $21,117! So, for borrowing $8,123 on credit cards, borrowers will pay back the $8,123 plus $12,994 interest! Notice that the interest cost is substantially greater than the original amount borrowed! That's crazy, any way you look at it!

Although debt has become the norm in our society, it is not the norm, according to God's principles of finance. In Deuteronomy 15:6; Psalm 37:21; and Romans 13:8, debt, especially long-term debt, is considered abnormal. Solomon wrote, "The rich rules over the poor, and the borrower becomes the lender's slave" (Proverbs 22:7). The Bible doesn't say that being in debt is sinful, but it does say that being in debt is tantamount to being a slave. The new slave masters of today are Visa (which should stand for Volunteering for Institutional Slavery Always), MassaCard (I'm sorry, I meant MasterCard), and Discover, to name a few!

What can you do to break the debt cycle? I believe with desire, discipline, time, and God's help, you can become debt free and stay that way, forever.

What can you do if you're already in debt? What can you do to break the debt cycle? I believe with desire, discipline, time, and God's help, you can become debt free and stay that way.

CHALLENGES AND SOLUTIONS

Challenge

I really want to get out of debt, but how do I start the process? I have so much debt that it seems like I'll never be able to pay it off.

Solution

You can get out of debt even though it may seem impossible for you right now. A lot of people just like you were once saddled with bills, but they are now debt free! It will take a lot of hard work, but as I said before, with God's help you can get out of debt. Here are some things you can do start the process:

- *Repent.* Ask God to forgive you for acquiring debts you know you shouldn't have incurred. He will forgive you and has the power to miraculously help you eliminate debt quickly (see 2 Kings 4:1–7).

- *Give the Lord His piece of the pie.* If you are not committed to giving God the tithe of your income, why should He be committed to helping you with your debt reduction plan? Withholding tithes from God indicates that you have not completely surrendered your finances to Him. In essence you are denying God the opportunity to bring His power into your situation.

- *Just say no to debt!* Buy what you can afford, not what you wish you could afford. The only surefire way to stop accumulating debt is to cut up your existing credit cards and pay for everything with cash, check, or debit cards. Just go cold turkey! Most people get into trouble with debt because they have too many credit cards. Stop letting the world system seduce you into thinking that you have to use debt in order to survive. Learn how to trust God and rely on His provision, rather than on credit and borrowing. The apostle Paul wrote, "I have learned to be content in whatever circumstances I am" (Philippians 4:11). You see, we are not born content; rather we learn contentment.

- *Drastically change your lifestyle.* The prophet Elisha asked the widow woman, who was deeply in debt, what she had in her house. She only had a little jar of oil, but that oil was the key to her freedom from debt! (See 2 Kings 4:1–7.) Look at your external assets and determine what you can turn into cash and apply toward the debts you owe. It may require selling your house, car, golf clubs, or motorcycle. No matter what it is, just be willing to do it.

Also, look at your internal assets, the God-given abilities and ideas that have been lying dormant inside of you for years! Sometimes the key to a financial breakthrough is determined by your obedience to God in the little things. Has the Lord been nudging you to start your own business, change companies, go into sales, etc.? Plant yourself in the right soil so you can prosper.

- *Develop a realistic spending plan (budget).* The reason a budget will help you get out of debt is because it will help you eliminate waste. I've seen people discover money they didn't know they had, after activating a spending plan. A written budget helps you plan ahead, discover wasteful spending patterns, and control the biggest budget buster of them all—impulse spending.

- *Start paying off debts a little at a time.* Begin by first paying extra on the debts that are the smallest and watch them disappear. Maintain the minimum payments on everything else, but put as much as you can toward the smaller debts. Once your lowest debt has been paid, apply the regular payment as well as the extra money that was going to the old debt toward the next highest bill you owe. After the second one is paid off, apply what was being paid on the first and second to the third highest, and so forth. Before you know it, your debts will disappear. Use the "Debt List" (page 228) to show every creditor, and balance due (as well as monthly payments and scheduled pay off dates) and, beginning with the lowest balances, start paying off those debts.

Challenge

Should I focus on getting out of debt or on saving money? I can probably do one, but achieving both at the same time seems impossible.

Solution

Getting out of debt is just like saving money. Let's say you have a $10,000 investment and it earns 10 percent, making you $1,000 richer. But suppose you also have $10,000 in credit card debt and your interest rate is 18 percent—that means you're paying $1,800 a year in interest. It doesn't take a math whiz to figure out that earning interest at 10 percent and paying interest at 18 percent is a net loss of capital ($1,000 interest earned minus $1,800 interest paid equals $800 capital loss). That's why getting out of debt is important; the more debt you have, the less your wealth will grow, even if you have other investments.

Although eliminating your debt is a priority, saving money is also important. There are two things you must absolutely do while you're getting out of debt: (1) save $1,000 or more toward a "rainy-day" fund (an emergency fund that will keep you from having to use a credit card when the car breaks down or when there's some other unexpected expense); and (2) contribute enough money to your company-sponsored 401(k) to qualify for the company match (if there is one). Taking advantage of matching funds is like getting free money, so don't pass it up. Once you've reached your contribution limit, apply the amount you were contributing toward your debts.

Challenge

Should I get a home equity loan to pay off my credit card debt? I'm in credit card debt up to my eyeballs and I was thinking of using some of the equity in my home to get more cash.

Solution

This may seem to make good financial sense in the short run, but in the long run, it's not. The reason it makes sense in the short run is because you can get a better home equity loan rate than what you are paying on your credit cards. If you itemize your deductions, the home equity loan is deductible on your income tax. So effectively, you end up paying much less on the home equity loan than you would if the debt was still on the credit cards. That's a good thing.

What I don't like is when you borrow against your home, your payments can be extended for a longer period of time, meaning that you are paying less interest initially, but over time you may be paying more in absolute dollars. Therefore, if you eliminate $20,000 of credit card debt by paying it off with a fifteen-year home equity loan, in the long run you may end up paying just as much as you would if you had kept it on the credit card. It's really a case of short-term gain and long-term pain.

Also, I don't like to see *unsecured* debt transferred to *secured* debt. Let me explain: a credit card is unsecured debt. The worst thing that can happen to you if you don't pay on your credit card is that your credit rating will go down. That's it. However, your house is a secured debt. If you don't pay the mortgage, you could end up homeless! Simply put, you're putting your house at risk when you use a home equity loan to pay off credit cards.

Lastly, and most importantly, for most people, using a home equity loan to pay off credit cards is like putting a Band-Aid on a bullet wound! Unless you get to the root of the problem (which most people don't), it's easy to end up right back in credit card debt again! Seventy percent of Americans who take out a home equity loan or another type of loan to pay off credit cards end up with the same, if not higher, debt load within two years. You end up with high credit cards to pay as well as the home equity loan. That combination is a recipe for foreclosure; I've seen it happen time and time again. People think borrowing on a home equity loan will solve their problem, but the problem was them, not the credit card debt!

Challenge

What kind of debt is good debt, and what kind of debt is bad? It doesn't seem possible not to have any debt at all or to pay cash for everything.

Solution

The Bible doesn't say that debt is a sin, yet it definitely discourages it. I just have a problem calling any debt good. Nowhere in the Bible is debt referred to as something good; therefore, I don't think there is any such thing as good debt. I prefer to call it acceptable debt versus unacceptable debt. By the way, all debt is dangerous and expensive. When you incur debt of any kind, you are *choosing* to pay a higher price for everything you buy because you are paying the purchase price plus interest!

Here's what I consider acceptable debt (and why):

1. *Mortgage loans.* This type of debt has the potential to appreciate or to produce income. In addition, the value of most real estate equals or exceeds the amount owed against it.
2. *Business loans.* These loans also have the potential to appreciate or to produce income. Plus, the value of the business has the potential to equal or exceed the amount owed against it.
3. *Educational loans.* Consider these an investment. Earning an undergraduate, graduate, or professional degree positions you to earn significantly more money than you would if you did not have the degree.

Now for unacceptable debt:

1. *Credit cards.* They can be addictive and most people tend to abuse this type of credit. The system makes it easy to get deeper in debt, to become a slave to debt, to spend money without considering the consequences, and to live above your means.
2. *Consumer goods.* Food, clothing, furniture, living essentials, etc., should not be bought on credit. Most of these types of items don't last long and you could be left paying for something you've already consumed or no longer use.
3. *Depreciating assets.* This applies primarily to automobiles. It is very easy to owe more on a car than it's worth (that's called, appropriately, being upside down). You may have a car note now, but pay the thing off and keep the car for five or more additional years (before you get back in debt purchasing a new one). You don't always have to have a car note. With a budget in place, you could soon be able to pay for your next car with cash!

Challenge

Isn't a credit card a necessity? It's almost impossible to rent a car, check into a hotel, book a flight, or to buy products online without a credit card. Besides, I heard that debit cards are riskier.

Solution

A credit card is not *a necessity.* A debit card or check card that is connected to your checking account gives you the ability to do virtually anything you can do with a credit card. Some rental car places don't take debit cards, but most do. You just have to do a little extra research to find them. The thing I like most about a debit card is that *it won't get you into debt!* Debit cards force you to be more responsible with your money since you can't spend what you don't have. There is no additional risk with a debit card. Over the last seven years or so, the debit card has been afforded the same protections in case of theft or fraud as a credit card.

MONEY FACT

An average of 60 percent of cardholders don't pay off their credit cards each month.

Challenge

Is there such a thing as a smart way to use credit cards? I think I'm pretty responsible with my credit cards. I pay them off at the end of each month and I take advantage of rebates and other perks.

Solution

Yes, there is a smart way to use credit cards; the trouble is that most people don't use them wisely. Financial expert Dave Ramsey says, "Responsible use of a credit card does not exist!" The more people I counsel financially, the more I tend to agree with Dave. Also, consider this: Studies have shown that even those who use credit cards "responsibly" still end up spending 12 to 18 percent *more* than had they used cash. That's money that could have been saved or spent to purchase other items. Psychologically, there's something about paying cash that hurts! First of all, credit cards are a piece of plastic instead of cash. Secondly, when using credit cards, we don't see the money we're spending.

Challenge

Does it help to transfer one credit card balance to another in order to get a lower rate? I received an offer in the mail to transfer my balance to another card with a lower rate. My current credit card rate is very high so this offer sounds appealing.

Solution

If you have halfway decent credit, your mailbox probably gets flooded daily with offers for low-interest credit card balance transfers. Some go as low as 0 percent and are hard to resist. A caution, however: Read the fine print before you leap. You could end up paying more than you would have if you'd just stayed put.

I'd like to refer you to a few questions that the Web site bankrate.com recommends you ask *before* making the decision to transfer your credit card balance:

- *How long does the rate last?* Typically, introductory "teaser" rates last six months, and occasionally a year, although some last for the life of the transfer. Be sure you know the details of the offer and how you intend to pay off your transferred debt. If you can pay it off during the teaser rate time frame, it might be a good deal. If not, think twice.

- *What are the minimum requirements to keep the low rate?* Even a 0 percent rate may come with a price. Some cards may require you to make a purchase every month to keep the low rate. Steer clear of cards that say they can raise your rate if they determine that your account "carries risk."

- *What's the interest rate for new purchases?* It might be the same low rate as the transfer, but don't count on it. If the rate is higher, you may also find yourself in for a shock when you begin to make payments. If you transfer a balance to a new card, it should be a card you don't plan to use.

- *Is there a balance-transfer fee?* Typically, cards charge about 3 percent of the transfer, up to $50 or $75 for making the transfer. So, while you may be getting a lower rate, you also incur an additional charge to your account. Add that into the interest rate you're getting to see if it will correlate into savings over time.

- *What will the rate be when it finally changes?* When you're dealing with balance transfers, you're really gambling. If the initial rate increases after a designated period of time, you'll soon be shopping for an equal or better rate when the rate changes. In today's rising interest rate environment, you may not be able to find a lower rate when you need it.

- *What about new purchases?* Unlike cash advances and balance transfers, purchases charged to the card will typically have a grace period before interest starts accruing.

- *Do you qualify for the lowest rate?* If you're someone who has credit card debt, you may not be a preferred customer. This means you won't get the best rates, so be sure to double-check everything when you get your card. The company may offer you a different rate if you don't qualify for the advertised rate used to hook you. Fortunately, you can cancel the card without penalty if you discover that you didn't get what you bargained for.

- *How is your information protected?* This is a key question for anyone to ask when applying for a card, but for those already in debt, it's particularly important. With hackers finding new ways to access personal account information, you'll want to make sure your credit card company will protect you so you don't have to deal with the hassle of identity theft on top of everything else.

Challenge

Should I use one of those debt consolidation companies to clean up my credit? I keep seeing debt consolidation commercials on TV and they sound pretty helpful.

Solution

You cannot borrow your way out of debt! When something sounds too good to be true, it usually is! Bestselling author Dave

Ramsey calls it Debt CONsolidation, because most of these companies are trying to con you! There are a lot of swindlers out there, but I know a few people who consolidated their debt, changed their habits, stuck to a budget, and ended up paying off the debt quicker. I'm not against debt consolidation, but be sure to work with a very reputable company like Consumer Credit Counseling.

Unfortunately, a lot of the companies that advertise on TV are not good. They claim to clean up your credit, but here's what they don't tell you:

- When it comes to acquiring a mortgage, debt consolidations that take your money and pay your bills will reflect on your credit as if you filed a chapter 13 bankruptcy.

- The only transactions that can be removed from your credit report are reporting errors or items that are seven years or older. Any company that tells you otherwise is either doing something illegal or flat-out lying!

Challenge

Is it wise to take advantage of a "90 day same-as-cash" deal? I want a flat-screen TV just like the one my neighbor has, but I can't afford it unless I take the ninety-day plan.

Solution

A large majority of people, 88 percent, who do these "90 day same-as-cash" deals *don't* pay them off in the allotted time. We all start off with good intentions, but somewhere down the line the game plan changes and we end up spending more than we bargained for. These deals have exploded over the past ten years. Every time I look around I see one advertised by a furniture, electronics, or appliance store. There are two primary reasons merchants offer these "teaser deals," or should I say "traps." Number one: Consumers are more inclined to buy more things when they are offered these kinds of deals. And when we buy more things, the stores make more money! Now the next one is the real reason these offers remain popular. When you fail to pay the bill within ninety days, *the contract converts to debt and you are charged a loan-shark rate*—between 24 percent and 38 percent from the date of the purchase! Now we're getting to the real bottom line of the retailers.

When you do a ninety-day same-as-cash contract, you are playing with fire and, according to the statistics, you will get burned! I've seen very few instances where the debt is paid in ninety days, so unless you know, with absolute certainty, that you can pay it off in the allotted time, don't do it!

Challenge

I cosigned for a friend, now I want out of the deal, but I don't know what to do. I thought I was doing the Christian thing by helping a friend in need, but it's adversely affecting my credit.

Solution

I think Proverbs 6:1–5 says it all:

> My child, if you co-sign a loan for a friend or guarantee the debt of someone you hardly know—if you have trapped yourself by your agreement and are caught by what you said —quick, get out of it if you possibly can! You have placed yourself at your friend's mercy. Now swallow your pride; go and beg to have your name erased. Don't put it off. Do it now! Don't rest until you do. Save yourself like a deer escaping from a hunter, like a bird fleeing from a net (NLT).

In other words, *get your name off of that loan quickly!*

It's your credit and you have the right to control it. You should ask the primary signer of the loan to try to refinance it with someone else as the cosigner. Of course they'll have to find a person willing to do this for them, but that's not your problem.

Challenge

I loaned a good friend some money and I'm very upset that they haven't paid me back. How should I handle the situation?

Solution

You should never loan money that you can't afford to lose. As a matter of fact, apart from rare occasions, you should never *loan* money at all but rather *give* to people when they need it.

One of the quickest ways to destroy a good relationship is to loan out money. There is certainly nothing wrong with loaning a good friend or family member money, but in doing so, you put the relationship at risk. Suppose they can't pay you back when they said they would? Suppose they don't pay you back at all? It would probably have an adverse affect on your relationship.

I recommend that you talk to the person and make sure he or she understands it was a loan. Next, ask the individual to explain why the loan hasn't been repaid and when you can expect to see the money. If the person says you probably won't see the money before you see Jesus, then you need to do one of two things: (1) work out a payment plan ($5, $10, $25 a week), or (2) forgive the loan. In most situations it's better to forgive the loan. When someone owes you money, they become a slave to you. (Remember, "The borrower becomes the lender's slave" [Proverbs 22:7].) If you want to be a true blessing to someone, ask the Lord how much you can afford to give him or her, instead of *loaning* the person money. That way, the person owes you nothing . . . but love.

Challenge

How do I handle the constant calls from collections people? I'm afraid to answer the phone anymore because I know it's going to be a creditor harassing me about bills I can't pay.

Solution

Collections people can be a pain to deal with, but not all of them are bad. Believe it or not some play by the rules. Keep in mind they're just trying to do their job, which is to collect on the money they believe you legally owe them. There is nothing wrong with that. If a company calls and wants to know when you're going to cough up the dough, you need to talk to them. Don't disguise your voice; don't pretend to be someone else and tell them you're not at home! Let them know when they can expect their money. Now, if they're mean and rude, that's another story. A lot of collectors will resort to whatever it takes to get you to ante up because they get paid by making you pay. They want to get you angry, emotional, upset, and even crying because they know that the more pressure they can put on you, the more likely you'll pay up just to get them off your back.

I am not teaching you to dodge your creditors, but don't let them manipulate you. Tell them how much you can pay and when you can pay them, then leave it at that. There's no need for long, combative, or disrespectful conversations (this is not the time to forget you are a Christian). When you agree to a special plan, deal, or settlement offer, get it in writing before you send any money!

Familiarize yourself with the Fair Debt Collection Practices Act (FDCPA), a federal law that dictates how and when a debt collector may contact you. A debt collector may not call you before 8 A.M. or after 8 P.M. or at work if you've told them your employer doesn't approve of the calls. Collectors may not harass you, make false statements, or use unfair practices when they try to collect a debt. Did you know you could ask them to stop calling you? Well, you can. Simply write a letter asking them to contact you in writing, instead of by phone. They are bound by law to honor your request, even if you owe them money.

TEN COMMANDMENTS FOR DEBT

1. Thou shall stop creating new debt.

2. Thou shall completely eliminate credit card debt.

3. Thou shall start purchasing things with cash and debit cards.

4. Thou shall check thy credit report at least once a year.

5. Thou shall avoid credit repair companies.

6. Thou shall use debt elimination as thy first and best investment.

7. Thou shall pay bills on time (pay more than the minimum payment).

8. Thou shall not file for bankruptcy.

9. Thou shall not cosign for a loan.

10. Thou shall use internal and external assets to pay off thy debts.

PRAYER

Dear Lord, I believe that it is Your will for me to prosper and not be bound by the chains of debt. You said if we delight ourselves in You that You will give us the desires of our heart. Therefore, Lord, I pray that You will help me to become completely debt free. Help me not to be seduced and controlled any longer by the power of debt. Father, I declare in Jesus' name, that my family and I will become debt free! We will be the head and not the tail; the lender and not the borrower. I humbly ask for Your forgiveness for the things I have done to cause me to be in so much debt. Give me wisdom as to how to get out of my debt. In the mighty name of Jesus I pray. Amen.

GIVING

THE REAL DEAL ABOUT GIVING

Salvation is free, but ministry's gonna cost you! In other words, it takes money to effectively operate a church and its ministries.

This reminds me of a conversation a Christian family had about their church. One family member said, "It's always hot in the church and the air conditioner hardly ever works." Another one said, "The gravel in the parking lot is killing my high-heel shoes. When are they gonna pave the darn thing?" Still another one said, "The choir and musicians sound terrible; the piano is always out of tune and everybody sings off key."

Finally Dad stood up and said, "I can't take it anymore! I'm sick and tired of hearing all this complaining. What do you expect for a dollar?"

This story illustrates a serious issue: You can't nickel and dime the Lord's house and expect to have a quality ministry, yet so many people do.

I talk to pastors of large and small congregations all over the country and more often than not I hear them say, "If most of my congregation would just give to their potential, our ministry could really impact the city . . . we could expand our facilities, pay off debt, clothe the naked, and feed the hungry. We could really fulfill the vision that God has given us." They say this because in most churches only between 20 to 30 percent of the congregation actually tithes. What's up with that?

Cirrhosis of the Giver (COG) is what's up. This disease is running unchecked through too many of our churches. The funny thing about COG is that it only seems to show up in church. For some reason wallets magically expand when it's time to buy an Escalade, a flat-screen TV, alligator shoes, or a beautiful dress! It's as if the disease goes into remission when you walk into a shopping mall, electronics store, or car dealership.

Take this quick in-home (or in-car, in-church, in-store) test to see if you have Cirrhosis of the Giver:

- Do you experience sudden paralysis and inability to reach for your wallet or purse when the offering plate comes your way?
- Do you "clam up" when the preacher talks about tithing and other donations?
- Do you find yourself sweating or getting mad at the preacher for talking about money?
- Do you pay everybody else before you pay God?

If you said "yes" or "sometimes" to any of these questions, then you've got it, baby! And if you're not careful, you could end up like Ananias and Sapphira did back in AD 34. They got greedy with God's gifts and suffered the consequences. (Don't take my word for it; read Acts 5:1–11.)

By failing to tithe, you are cheating God, His kingdom, and yourself. Imagine the miraculous work that could be done if you and all the members of your church tithed. A Christian school could be built, a business development program could be launched, and a health care or financial training ministry could be created.

COG is a killer disease, crushing large and small churches across the country. Check out these statistics from the Empty Tomb and Christian Stewardship Associations:

- The average Christian in America gives only 2.5 percent of his or her income to the kingdom of God.

- The percentage Christians give financially to God has been declining for the past twenty-six years.

- A huge 97 percent of pastors feel that while people's income has increased, their giving has not.

- Between 80 percent and 90 percent of Christians do not give 10 percent or more. (In other words, most church folks don't tithe!)

- The giving records of between 30 percent and 50 percent of church attendees are blank. (These churchgoers didn't give God a single dime!)

The statistics are staggering, yet this disease can be eradicated. God can cure you of all your ailments, including Cirrhosis of the Giver.

"Remember the words of the Lord Jesus, that He Himself said, 'It is more blessed to give than to receive'" (Acts 20:35). So the next time you feel hesitant about giving back to God, replace your fear with faith and remember that God has promised to take care of your needs. Open your heart to God, obey His Word, and you will be rewarded.

CHALLENGES AND SOLUTIONS

Challenge

Since Christians are under grace, not under law, does the obligation to tithe still apply to us? I've had friends tell me that tithing is Old Testament law and is not relevant to the New Testament believer.

Solution

Although I'm not a theologian (I'm a financial guy), I'll try to answer this controversial question the best that I can (although it would take the entire book to adequately prove my point).

First of all, the distinction of law/grace and Old Testament/New Testament in Scripture is often misused, partly because the teaching is difficult to understand, but also because when it comes to money, most people tend to seek out ways to dodge obedience. It is certainly true that Christians are under the principle of grace, not the principle of law. In other words, we attain righteousness not by our works but by the grace of God. However, being under grace does not mean living by lower standards or giving less to God. On the contrary, it means giving and doing more. In the New Testament when Jesus dealt with issues like adultery and murder (to name a few), He never lowered the bar; He always raised it (Matthew 5:17–48). In my experience, I have found that many people who argue against tithing use their arguments to justify their own lack of generosity. They simply don't want to give that much and they use the law/grace issue as an excuse.

Concerning the New Testament/Old Testament issue, where in the New Testament does it indicate that tithing is no longer valid? Last time I checked, there is no such passage. In the New Testament we are never told that tithing has been annulled or canceled. As a matter of fact, Jesus directly affirmed it in Matthew 23:23. We must be careful not to throw out the baby (ongoing principles intended for everyone) with the bathwater (detailed regulations intended only for ancient Israel). In my opinion, tithing is still relevant for the New Testament believer. It isn't the finish line of giving; it's the starting block!

Challenge

What's the difference between tithes, freewill offerings, and first-fruits? It seems like there's an offering for everything and it's got me a little confused.

Solution

Your giving options can be confusing, so let me try to "make it plain." First of all, *tithing* means "tenth part." Many people erroneously ascribe tithing to all of their Christian giving. They may earn $500 a week and say, "I tithed $10 this week." Well, since a tithe means "tenth," they didn't actually tithe, they *donated* $10. A tithe would have been $50. In my opinion, God expects Christians to tithe since the money we earn belongs to Him.

Freewill offerings, on the other hand, are what you give *over and above* the tithe. These offerings are voluntary, given out of joy, love, and worship. Simply put, you give offerings because you want to. Now don't get me wrong; giving voluntary offerings is not optional for the Christian. One of the reasons the Israelites were rebuked by God in Malachi 3 was because they were robbing Him of their tithes *and offerings*.

Whereas the tithe refers to the *quantity* of what you give, *first-fruits* refers to the *quality* of what you give. Your tithe is actually a form of *"first fruits"* (Leviticus 23:17). Giving God the first 10 percent of your goods means you trust Him to stretch the other 90 percent to meet your needs (Proverbs 3:9–10). The tithe should be "taken off the top" and is considered the first and best of what you have to offer the Lord.

There are quite a few people teaching about *firstfruits offerings* these days, especially in charismatic circles. They interpret this kind of offering as completely separate from the tithe. I believe this is a legitimate biblical principle; however, I've seen a lot of confusion and abuse surrounding this issue. A firstfruits offering is actually a type of freewill offering that is typically

MONEY FACT

Did you know that tycoon John D. Rockefeller tithed? He once revealed, "I never would have been able to tithe on my first million dollars if I had not learned to tithe on my first paycheck, which was $1.50 for the week."

given at the beginning of the year (although it doesn't matter when you give it). People who give this type of offering do it because they believe it is a "financial seed," representative of the anticipated harvest they desire and expect to receive from God (over a certain time frame). Again, I have no problem with the principle in general, but I don't think it's appropriate to make firstfruits offerings mandatory. In some churches, members are cajoled, pressured, and made to feel guilty if they don't participate. Secondly, you can't manipulate God into blessing you financially.

There is no so-called "formula" that we can use to get God to prosper us. Sometimes people use firstfruits offerings as a kind of crowbar to try to twist God's arm into blessing them financially. Even worse, some churches use it as another "gimmick" to raise more money. Even a good principle can become contaminated when people's motives are wrong. I'm afraid that's what I've seen, more often than not, concerning firstfruits offerings.

Challenge

Won't God understand if I don't tithe? He knows exactly how many bills I've got to pay and how little money I have, so I think He should understand my dilemma.

Solution

Of course God understands. He understands that you could tithe if you really wanted to! Most people I have counseled testify that they live just as easily on 90 percent of their income as they did on 100 percent. Be honest with yourself. Is it that you can't afford to tithe or that you prefer to put your tithe on your back (clothes), in your garage (cars), or on your feet (shoes), instead of in the collection plate? Hey, don't get mad at me; I'm just calling it like I see it.

Remember, tithing is God's will and He promises to provide for those who trust and obey Him. It's been my experience that when we stop trusting and obeying God (by starting to withhold our tithes), our financial problems arise. In other words, when you rob God, you rob yourself of God's blessings. Start tithing regularly, and you'll realize that it's a lot safer living on less inside the will of God than living on more outside of it.

Challenge

Is it OK to refrain from giving to the church if you don't agree with where the money goes? I disagree with how my church leaders handle the money, therefore I choose not to tithe.

Solution

No, it is not OK. When you give your money to the church, you are actually giving to the Lord. God will honor your obedience to Him regardless of what happens to the money once it leaves your hands. Even if a pastor, deacon, or elder runs off with the offering money and gambles it away in Las Vegas, God will still bless *you* for your obedience.

Yes, God expects you to give and to give responsibly, and you should want to plant in good ground. Here's my first question for you: "Are your concerns for real or is this just an excuse to hold on to your cash?" If you really don't trust your church leaders with God's money, then ask yourself, "Do my church leaders need to repent of their greed (which is possible), or do I need to repent of my own attitude toward them (which is also very likely)?" Remember it is not our place to impugn the motives of the pastor or other church leaders. If you are truly concerned that your church leaders are living in willful financial sin, then approach them about it (Matthew 18:15–20), instead of just withdrawing your money. If you can't get answers you can live with, then find another church you can trust and start tithing.

Challenge

Should I tithe my gross or net income? It seems only fair that I tithe based on what I actually take home.

Solution

In my opinion, the Word teaches that we are to give from our gross personal income, not our net. Remember, the quality of what we give to God is just as important as the quantity. Proverbs 3:9 states, "Honor the LORD from your wealth and from the first of all your produce." I interpret "from the first" to mean that we should give from our gross income.

Giving a tithe from your net income (after you've paid your taxes and other deductions) means that you're not giving God your absolute best. In the Old Testament, the Israelites were committed to giving God 10 percent because to do anything less was to "rob God." They believed that whatever God provided them in the form of materials or cash or benefits of any sort, 10 percent of it belonged to Him. They gave to God from the top (gross amount), not from the bottom.

But don't get all bent out of shape on this issue. If you don't have the conviction or faith to tithe based on your gross income, then go ahead and tithe from your net income. Just remember the words that an old preacher told me a long time ago, "Whether you tithe off the gross or the net depends on whether you want a gross or net blessing." I don't know about you, but I want a blessing on everything I produce. I want a blessing from my gross!

Challenge

Can I tithe my time rather than tithing money to my church? They say, "Time is money," and I give up a lot of time at church; it ought to be worth something.

Solution

Of course you can tithe your time, but not in lieu of tithing your money. Jesus said, "For where your treasure is, there your heart will be also" (Matthew 6:21). Notice He didn't say, "where your time is." Money is an indicator of where our hearts really are. The great evangelist Billy Graham said, "Our checkbooks are our theological documents. They tell us what we truly worship."

After I had preached about giving at a church one evening, one of the deacons of the church drove me back to my hotel. On the way he told me that he didn't tithe his money to his church but that he volunteered his time. According to him, giving his time was just as good as giving money. I said, "Hogwash!" I told him he was just being stingy with his money and didn't want to let any of it go. After a couple of seconds of silence (which seemed like an eternity), he said, "Man, you know what, you're right. I'm just looking for some excuses." The man even thanked me for challenging him on his thrifty habits.

Challenge

Is it OK to give some of my tithe money to family and friends who need financial assistance? The way I see it, my family needs the money more than the church.

Solution

First of all, your church needs money too! Remember, salvation is free but ministry is expensive! God says, "Bring the whole tithe into the storehouse, so that there may be food in My house" (Malachi 3:10). In the Old Testament there was a storehouse in the sanctuary, built for depositing the tithes and offerings of the people. The New Testament counterpart of this principle is that the church members give all their tithes to the local church.

"Storehouse tithing" means to bring your tithes to the church where your membership is established, your spiritual life is nourished, and your church privileges are enjoyed. If you give elsewhere, then it should be over and above the required tithe to your church, if at all possible.

However, there is certainly nothing wrong with you helping a loved one financially. If you have an elderly parent or a sibling in dire straits, I believe that it's okay to use some of your tithe money to assist them, but only if you absolutely have no other funds from which you can help them. Also, the assistance you give them should only be occasional and not a lifestyle. You could actually be hurting them by always bailing them out financially. Sometimes giving people money is not the solution to their problem. However, I do believe that God blesses us so we can be a blessing to others. Just be careful not to substitute what belongs in God's house by putting it in someone else's house. Don't ever forget who your source is.

> **MONEY FACT**
>
> The more money people make, the less they give. Those earning more than $100,000 gave 2.9 percent to charities; those with incomes under $10,000 gave 5.5 percent.

Challenge

I own my own business and don't know if I should tithe off the gross revenues of my business or just my personal income.

Solution

Tithes should come from personal income. If you feel led by God to tithe off of the gross revenues of your business, then go ahead and do so. However, business owners must pay for materials, rent, employee wages, and many other expenses. These costs are not included in their personal gross income and would not be subject to tithing.

Challenge

When should I introduce my children to tithing? I want them to get in the habit of tithing, but I'm not sure what age is appropriate.

Solution

Once children know the value of money, they should also know the value of giving. How can you tell? Put a $1 bill, a $5 bill, and a $10 bill on a table and ask your child to choose only one of the bills. If he/she chooses the $10 dollar bill, then it's time to teach them about giving and tithing. In our household, my wife and I taught our children about tithing at a very early age. Now that they are teenagers and have jobs of their own, the first thing they think of when they receive their paychecks is the percentage of money they will give to the Lord. Next, they calculate the percentage they will save and the percentage they will spend. If you teach your children to tithe when they are receiving an allowance, they will still tithe when they are receiving a paycheck. It's also important to point out their blessings from the Lord because of their giving. As a parent, I find that I even want to personally bless my children more because of their giving hearts.

Challenge

If I give 10 percent of my income to God, can I do what I want with the 90 percent I have left?

Solution

No, because it all belongs to God—the entire 100 percent! It is important to give 10 percent as a tithe, but it is just as important to be a good steward of the remaining 90 percent. Remember, God owns it all (1 Chronicles 29:11). God expects us to be responsible with the resources that He has blessed us with. If you are a faithful tither, but mismanage the rest of your money, then you will never experience the full blessings of the tithe. That's why it is important to have a budget so you can responsibly manage all the money God bestows upon you.

Challenge

Where should my tithe go when I don't have a church home? We left our former church and are currently looking for a new church home. Should we give our tithes to the old church, the churches we visit or just wait until we join a new one?

Solution

Always honor the man or woman of God who feeds you spiritually. By all means, go ahead and give your tithes to the church or churches you are visiting, until you find a new church home.

I want to commend you for your desire to remain faithful to God in your giving, even while you are in between churches. A lot of people cease their tithing until they find a new church. I know of some instances where it took a family six months, or even up to a year, to find a new church home and they ceased tithing during that time. I don't believe that is wise. Wherever you're getting fed is where you should tithe. It could be a church you are visiting, or a ministry that is impacting you on the radio, TV, or even a parachurch ministry. "Elders who do their work well should be paid well, especially those who work hard at both preaching and teaching," wrote the apostle Paul (1 Timothy 5:17 NLT).

TEN COMMANDMENTS FOR GIVING

1. Thou shall honor the Lord with thy tithe (10 percent of gross income).

2. Thou shall give freewill offerings to the Lord (over and above the tithe).

3. Thou shall give with the right attitude and motivation.

4. Thou shall be a good steward with the remaining 90 percent of income.

5. Thou shall teach thy children about giving as soon as they understand the value of a dollar.

6. Thou shall give to family and friends, if led by the Holy Spirit.

7. Thou shall give to the person/place that feeds thee spiritually (even while searching for a new church home).

8. Thou shall give to the poor and widowed.

9. Thou shall give in good soil (a good church).

10. Thou shall test God in the area of giving. Then you'll really see how faithful God is.

PRAYER

Dear Lord, I want to experience the joy of giving, and I believe Your Word when it says, "It is more blessed to give than to receive." As an outward expression of my commitment to You, I honor You with my substance and the firstfruits of all my produce. Lord, I trust You with my finances and I believe that You can do more for me as I live on 90 percent of my income, than I could do for myself living on 100 percent of my income. Therefore Lord, help me to be obedient in the area of giving. Help me to honor You with my tithes and offerings.

As I give Lord, I pray that You will change me from the inside out. Give me a generous heart and help me to be sensitive to the needs of others, especially the poor. Mold my character and my attitude and help me to always keep Your kingdom first. Lord, I pray that as I am faithful in the area of giving, You will open up the windows of heaven and pour out a blessing that there shall not be room enough to receive it. Rebuke the Enemy and any destructive force that tries to affect my financial success. From now on, I hold everything that I have with an open hand. I surrender all I have to You because it all belongs to You. Help me to be a generous giver so that Your kingdom can be established. In Jesus' mighty name I pray. Amen.

ROMANCE AND FINANCE

THE REAL DEAL ABOUT ROMANCE AND FINANCE

Sometimes opposites don't attract—they attack! While waiting for a plane to depart, I overheard two female passengers talking. The younger woman noticed that her new acquaintance wore a wedding ring on the middle finger, instead of the ring finger. Curious, the younger woman asked, "Why do you wear your wedding ring on the wrong finger?" The elder woman replied, rather abruptly, "Cause I married the wrong man!"

A whole lot of men and women feel like they married the wrong person once financial history, bad debts, and low bank account balances finally get revealed. It's not only the past, but differences in present and future money-management styles that can cause a rift in even the most loving households. When it comes to money matters, sometimes opposites don't attract; instead they *attack*!

Experts contend that money and sex are the topics that bring most people into counseling and are the topics couples find most difficult to discuss calmly. In fact, financial differences are the leading cause of marital discord today. According to the survey conducted by Consumer Credit Counseling Service, 60 percent of married respondents reported fighting about money with their spouse and more than 93 percent reported that financial problems increased the amount of stress in their lives.

What happened to living happily ever after? It's still possible, with honest and frequent communication. Without such communication you could find your money and your relationship bankrupt. In the midst of planning for the wedding and honeymoon, spend some time working on the household budget. I know, it's not as romantic as a moonlit stroll on the beach, but it could prevent a daylight dash to divorce court.

In Genesis 2:24 the Bible captures the essence of marriage, "Therefore shall a man leave his father and his mother and hold fast to his wife, and they shall become one flesh" (ESV). These three things—*leave*, *cleave*, and *become one*—involve every aspect of the marital relationship, including money. Although most people have heard these words, many don't know what they mean. Let's talk about them from a financial perspective.

The first step in marriage is for the man to *leave* his father and mother. If you're living in your mother's basement, borrowing your daddy's car, or still collecting an allowance from your folks, you ain't ready to get married. When a man is prepared to marry a woman, he is totally self-sufficient and equipped to lead his own household.

Secondly, a husband must *cleave* to his wife. In other words, the brother's gonna "stick like glue" or hang on as tight as he can to his new spouse. This expression "hold fast to" transcends the physical union with the body and represents a union with the whole person. Brothers, when you say, "I do," you proclaim that everything you possess is shared with your spouse; there's no more "mine" but "ours." Your new job is to please, provide for, and care for your wife. In doing so, you fulfill one of a woman's greatest needs in marriage—security.

Thirdly, God says if a man will leave and cleave, he and his wife will become *one flesh*. That's a promise. When you become one flesh, you may have different perspectives about money, but they become complementary rather than divisive. If one is a saver and the other a spender or one is conservative and the other a risk taker, a balance is found that allows you to move in unison toward the goal of building a fruitful and lifelong partnership. When you become one, the differences make the relationship better. You sharpen one another, cover each other's blind spots, and you bring fresh viewpoints, which lead to a better financial life where there's harmony instead of discord.

Within a marriage relationship the husband and wife are financial partners, dedicated to one another in times of feast and famine. They use God's Word, communication, and budgeting to master their money and their marriage.

CHALLENGES AND SOLUTIONS

Challenge

Is it a good idea for my boyfriend and me to move in together to save a few bucks? We love the Lord, but living together sure would take a load off my bank account. Who knows, we may even decide to get married.

Solution

"Shacking up" is *not* the solution to your financial problems! Yes, I know that's "old school," but it's also God's school. This whole "shacking up" thing is just an excuse that you and a lot of couples (even Christian couples) use to rationalize why they want to live in sin. Of course it makes economic sense; the Devil's wages always look better than God's! You said that you loved the Lord.

Well shacking up is the antithesis of what a Christian couple should be doing. Don't you want God to bless you? He can only do that if you do things His way.

Shacking up might enhance your bank account, but it could ruin your relationship. According to statistics, the divorce rate is higher for couples who live together before marriage than for those who don't. Then there's the challenge of untangling your financial lives. When a couple who cohabitates (lives together) breaks up, sometimes it can be just as messy as a divorce.

Instead of shacking, you and your boyfriend should stay in separate homes. If either one of you can't afford the apartment or house you live in, then get a roommate or move into a cheaper place. Next, get on a budget and watch where you put your money. (You may find a lot of ways to cut corners—that is if you really want to save money.) Then cut your expenses and/or increase your income. (A part-time job may help.) If you commit to doing things God's way, your situation will get better.

Challenge

When should my fiancé and I discuss finances? We're getting married in a few months and I don't want to rock the boat by bringing up money. Besides, I'm not really sure what questions to ask.

Solution

If you're planning to get married, you've got to talk about finances *before* you jump the broom or tie the knot. Otherwise you're setting your marriage up for failure.

Why is it so easy for couples to talk about how many kids they want, where they'll live, what church they'll attend, and which cars they want to own yet it's so painful to talk about the one thing they deal with every day—money? I've even had a few engaged couples tell me how "unromantic" the subject of money is!

Let me tell you, if you want long-lasting romance, you'd better talk about finances! How romantic will you feel huddled on the street while your home is being repossessed? The Scripture warns us, "Do not give the Devil an opportunity" (Ephesians 4:27). I guarantee, if you place your financial history in a closet, the Devil will open the door just to see how much havoc he can create. When you expose where you are to your fiancé *before* you get married, you don't allow the Devil to gain a foothold on your relationship.

Don't know what to ask? Start with these questions:

1. What are your financial assets and liabilities? (What do you own; what do you owe?)
2. What type of debt (credit card, auto loan, second mortgage, college loan, etc.) do you have? (This will give you a clue about how they use debt.)
3. What's your FICO score? (Couples must see and discuss each other's credit reports before they get married.)
4. Are you a tither? (Saying he/she "put five on it" does not make them a tither.)
5. What are your financial aspirations? (For example, to be debt-free in three years; accumulate $100,000 in stocks; or have a $25,000 savings account.)
6. What are your career expectations? (Buy a franchise; retire in ten years; become a stay-at-home mom in two years.
7. How do you propose we divide financial duties? (If the answer is "You make it, I spend it," grab your purse or your wallet and run for the hills!)
8. Will we operate from one checkbook, two, or three?
9. Do you have to take care of any family members financially? (You may discover there's a child, elderly parent, or sibling you didn't know about!)

MONEY FACT

An overwhelming 80 percent of those who divorce cite financial difficulties as the main cause.

These questions will give you a great start. Don't be surprised if you hear some things that shock you. Believe me, it's better to live with the pain of truth now, than the pain of regret later.

Challenge

Am I obligated to help my spouse pay off debt that I didn't bring into the marriage? I have very little debt; however, my fiancé has a ton of credit card debt and a school loan that I don't think I should have to pay.

Solution

As soon as you say, "I do," the debt your spouse brings into the marriage becomes YOUR responsibility too. (If he or she came in with a boatload of cash, you'd want them to share it, wouldn't you?) Don't forget what the Bible says, "A man shall leave his father and his mother and hold fast to his wife, and they shall become one flesh" (Genesis 2:24 ESV). That's "one flesh" spiritually, physically, and financially! So drop "mine" and "yours" from your vocabulary and get used to saying, "ours"—our money, our debt, our wealth.

Your responsibility as a committed spouse is to help lighten the burden for your mate, which will lighten the burden on your marriage. Sit down with your spouse, analyze your income and expenses; then come up with a plan to eradicate the debt. Share your technique for staying debt free; offer advice and support. If you work together, it can be done!

Also, keep in mind that if your spouse enters the marriage with bad credit, it affects both of you. In fact, you may be turned down for credit cards or loans that you apply for together if your spouse has had serious credit problems. The solution may be to seriously consider keeping your credit separate; at least until your spouse's credit record improves. You don't have to combine your credit when you marry. You can have separate "associate" cards issued for your spouse to use. Even if your spouse has bad credit, your credit rating will remain unaffected.

However, keeping separate credit can be problematic. You'll have a harder time qualifying for loans (especially a mortgage) by yourself versus having both incomes counted. Your spouse may also resent the fact that all the loans are in your name. This can be especially challenging when the wife controls the credit and the husband is the one with bad credit.

It's important not to let this situation ruin your relationship. You are here to help each other. That's what marriage is all about.

Challenge

Is it wrong to hide money from your spouse? I feel like I need to keep a little something on the side for a rainy day.

Solution

Yes, it is wrong. Hiding money from your marriage partner is an act of financial infidelity! There's more than one way to be unfaithful, and you've just hit on a big one. Dishonesty in a marriage is never good. The question is *why* do you feel like you have to hide money from your spouse? Was this taught to you by one of your parents, or has your spouse given you cause for distrust?

If you don't trust your partner, the issue needs to be addressed. Ask God for help and guidance. Talk to your spouse and seek counseling. If there's no basis for distrust and you're hiding money because someone told you to, stop it now. Keeping money secrets and separate accounts (that your spouse doesn't know about) will only eat away at your marriage. Before we got married, my mother-in-law even told my wife to keep a stash on the side! Fortunately, my wife chose to ignore the advice.

Reestablish open and honest communication with your

spouse, repent, and ask them for forgiveness. Most importantly, address whatever motivated you to start hiding money.

Challenge

Is it ever OK to have separate accounts? My spouse and I have a pretty good marriage. I think it's because we handle our money separately, but one of my church members says our marriage would be stronger if we combined our resources.

Solution

I'm glad you have a good marriage; however, you have been living like two single people within a marriage covenant and that's not how God designed marriage to be. I wonder why you wouldn't want to pool your assets. Unwillingness to join all assets and bank accounts in a marriage is perhaps a danger signal of unresolved trust issues. Of the couples I've advised over the last twenty years, those who pooled their resources and worked together as a team typically had more intimate and more fulfilling marriages than those who kept separate accounts. It's no wonder Ecclesiastes 4:9 (GNT) says, "Two are better off than one, because together they can work more effectively."

Genesis also talks about two becoming one in marriage (2:24), a process that is facilitated by doing things jointly instead of individually. Combining your finances creates an atmosphere to discuss money values and beliefs, express desired goals, and pay bills jointly. Another benefit is that no one will be in the dark about where the money is coming from or where it's going.

I suggest that you gradually start pooling your resources so that you don't get overwhelmed. It may feel awkward at first, but if you are both committed to the process, it will soon become second nature.

You also asked if it's ever OK to have separate accounts? Generally no, but there are extenuating circumstances. If you have a business account, then it is certainly appropriate to keep things separate from your personal accounts. Some couples I know establish small "mad money" accounts. These are small discretionary accounts that each spouse can spend in any way they choose. As long as there is an agreed upon amount and as long as there's transparency (no money is hidden), I have no problem with married couples having a little financial autonomy. Be careful not to forget that what belongs to one belongs to both.

Challenge

How should married people handle their differences when it comes to money? My spouse and I have completely different views on how to spend and save money and it's causing some major problems in our marriage.

Solution

You don't have to be the same, but you do have to be *on the same page*. Learn how to make those differences work for you instead of against you. No one ever said you had to be exactly alike in order to have a great marriage or financial life.

Believe that God joined the two of you to prosper. Christ has said, "The thief comes only to steal and kill and destroy; I came that they may have life, and have it abundantly" (John 10:10). Trust that your spouse is not the Enemy; Satan is. Then prepare yourself for spiritual warfare. This is why it is so important for married couples to pray with one another.

Secondly, don't be afraid to talk about your differences. If this leads to an argument or an impasse, then hire a marriage counselor or seek the advice of a wise, seasoned, married couple. Thirdly, and most importantly, both of you must be willing to compromise. Marriage only works when two people die to their own desires for the betterment of the marriage.

Challenge

How should a man deal with a wife who earns more money and won't let him forget it? I feel like my wife tries to emasculate me and it's wearing on my self-esteem and my love for her.

Solution

We've been conditioned to equate money with manhood, but that doesn't make it right. Therefore when the wife earns more money than the husband, it can sometimes create problems. Some women become more controlling and domineering when they become the primary breadwinner, while some men become insecure and overly sensitive, believing they are no longer the head honcho.

Recent research has found that marriages tend to be happier when men earn more. Yet, over the last twenty years or so, women's paychecks have moved close to and in some cases have surpassed men's pay, which is bound to affect male-female financial roles in marriage. Under these circumstances, it doesn't make sense to hold fast to traditional precepts; a little change is in order. Men and women need to adjust their hearts and minds in order to make this situation work.

Here are some suggestions for the woman with a "phat" paycheck who wants to maintain peace and harmony in the home:

- *Refrain from controlling and domineering behavior and dialogue.* Although your husband may earn significantly less, he is still the leader of the home and the man you swore to love and honor. Respect his authority and treat him with love.

- *Become his biggest cheerleader.* Tell your husband how proud you are of him and how much you appreciate what he does. You have to believe deep down that what your partner is bringing to the relationship is just as valuable as what you're bringing. If not, it won't work.

- *Make him feel like he's a part of your success.* None of us achieves success alone. Acknowledge your man's contributions to your success by complimenting him privately and bragging on him publicly. That way he fills like your success is his success too.

- *Refer to the money you earn as "ours" instead of "mine."* When you get a raise or bonus, talk about it within the context of your shared goals as a couple. "We got a raise! Look at what we can do now . . . pay off the house, travel, or buy a new car!" Submit the major financial decisions to him and resist the temptation to tell him what you're going to do.

Now some suggestions for the man whose woman brings home the bigger steak:

- *Get over the fact that she makes more money than you.* Earning less than your wife doesn't make you any less of a man. Your manhood is measured by a willingness to do your best, respect your wife, and follow God's Word. It's time to deal with any insecurity you might have before it ruins your marriage.

- *Become her biggest cheerleader.* Flood your wife with encouraging words and tell her how proud you are of her accomplishments. She needs to hear that from you more than anyone else.

- *Continue to be the spiritual leader of the home.* God doesn't care about the size of your paycheck. He fully expects you to fulfill your role as the household's spiritual leader; don't shirk your duties. Act like a leader, and your wife will respect you as a leader.

Challenge

My wife and I both agreed she would become a stay-at-home mother, but we're wondering how do we adjust to living on one income? I know "the Lord provides," but I have to admit I'm a little worried.

Solution

It's a noble thing to "bring your wife home," but without proper planning, it could be a financial nightmare. "Plan carefully and you will have plenty; if you act too quickly, you will never have enough" (Proverbs 21:5 GNT).

Did you know that the average credit card debt of the typical family *increases* when the wife comes home? This is primarily because the couple didn't plan properly and had to resort to credit cards to take up the slack. Quite often a wife who quits has to go back to work at some point because of the debt and the pressure the decision created. If your wife is thinking about leaving the workforce to raise your children, here's what you need to do:

1. *Start planning at least a year in advance.* You have to get acclimated to living on one income. The only way to do that is to start saving most of what she earns now, so you can have an adequate cash reserve when she quits. Set a goal of trying to save all of her income or at the very least half of it.

2. *Develop a realistic budget.* Since you'll only have one income, the question becomes, will one income be enough to sustain you? If the answer is no, then you'll need to make some tough decisions. First, you'll have to determine if it's the best time for your wife to quit her job. Maybe she needs to work a little longer, giving you time to save more money. Secondly, you may need to consider drastically altering your lifestyle to reduce expenses.

Challenge

Does the fact that my husband is the primary breadwinner give him the right to act like a financial dictator and disregard my opinions? He makes all of the financial decisions and even determines how much money I spend and what I'm allowed to spend it on.

Solution

Marriage is a partnership, not a dictatorship. In this instance, silence is not golden. The apostle Paul says wives should be submissive to their husbands, but that doesn't mean you should be muzzled. Your opinions and insights are just as important as your husband's, regardless of who brings home the bacon. Peter tells us, "Likewise, husbands live with your wives in an understanding way, showing honor to the woman as the weaker vessel, since they are heirs with you of the grace of life, so that your prayers may not be hindered" (1 Peter 3:7 ESV).

Peter wasn't suggesting that a wife is the weaker vessel mentally, morally, or spiritually but rather physically. (There are exceptions, of course, but generally speaking, men are physically stronger than women.) An accurate interpretation is that the husband should treat his wife like a valuable, beautiful, and fragile vase, in which there lies a precious treasure. A lot of husbands, who think they know it all, grossly underestimate the precious treasure (wisdom) that their wives possess. That's a shame, because in doing so they miss out on the joy and intimacy that comes along with making decisions together.

As a wife seeking to improve the situation, consider this:

- *He may not realize he's a financial dictator.* If that's the case, lovingly share your feelings with him. Try saying something like this: "I love you and I believe God created me to be your helpmate. I would like to be more involved with our finances, and I believe it's one of the ways I can help you and our family. When you make all of the financial decisions, and don't include me, I feel _____."

Let your husband know how it makes you feel, then try to find some common ground. Please understand that he may be acting out what he's seen his father do. This style of leadership may be all he knows. Some men mistakenly think that being a good leader means being dictatorial. Nothing could be further from the truth. Jesus was a gentle leader. He never crushed somebody else's spirit to assert His authority.

- *He may not realize how wise and talented you are.* I hate to admit this, but it took me a few years to appreciate my wife's wisdom. Early in our marriage I thought I knew everything! My wife would gently suggest things to me, but I was too hardheaded to listen. Mine was the way of the fool (see Proverbs 12:15). After a few stupid decisions I realized I needed to seek out and listen to my wife's counsel.

MONEY FACT

In general, women spend more frequently than men, but men spend a lot more because their toys cost more!

Challenge

Who should handle the daily finances like paying bills and balancing the checkbook? I've been told that this is the husband's responsibility as the "head of the house," but I'm a much better money manager than my husband.

Solution

It doesn't matter who handles the daily finances as long as the best person is doing it. Whoever is the best bookkeeper, the most detailed, and has the most time, should be the primary money manager of household finances. Just because the husband is the leader doesn't necessarily mean he has to write all the checks and pay all the bills. In the majority of cases, wives make better daily money managers than their husbands, but that's not always true.

I believe that the budget should be done together, but the day-to-day financial decisions can be done by one person (since it's a reflection of the budget anyway). If you're a better money manager than your husband, then I suggest that you handle the daily financial chores. Tell him it could help free up his time and assure him that you will keep him informed. He probably won't have a problem with it.

There is one exception when I think the husband should always handle the daily finances and that is when the family is experiencing severe financial problems. In my opinion, a husband should not put his wife under the daily pressures of juggling the bills and trying to make ends meet. When money is tight, it brings on more stress. The person who sees what's coming in and going out on a daily basis is usually the one who is stressed out the most. I believe it is the husband's duty as the leader to bear this burden, not the wife.

Challenge

Who has the final say regarding financial decisions in the home, the husband or the wife? As partners I think we should both agree, but my mother says I should let my husband make the final decisions, whether I agree with them or not.

Solution

In a good marriage, most financial decisions are made jointly, however, there's bound to be a time when the husband and wife are not in agreement. *When there is an impasse, the husband has the final say;* the wife should yield to her spouse and allow the Lord to work it out. Ladies, I know this is not easy, especially when you think you're right, but you must learn to trust God in these matters. The Bible says, "Wives, yield to your husbands, as you do to the Lord, because the husband is the head of the wife, as Christ is the head of the church. And He is the Savior of the body, which is the church. As the church yields to Christ, so you wives should yield to your husbands in everything" (Ephesians 5:22 NCV).

When you are not in agreement with something your husband wants to do, consider these three things:

1. *Let him know you disagree with him in a loving and respectful way.* It's all right to disagree with your spouse on some things. Just don't let the difference of opinion alienate you from one another.

2. *Ask him to get counsel regarding the matter.* Sometimes God may use another person to tell your husband the exact same thing you've been telling him. It's a shame, but when some men are told what to do by someone other than their wives, they receive it better.

3. *Pray and put it in God's hands.* God may give you insight or peace about the situation once you put it in His hands. He may even change your husband's heart! Prayer works wonders.

Challenge

How do you feel about a working wife and a stay-at-home husband? We can more than afford to live on my wife's income, which is much higher than mine. Plus, it'll give me a chance to stay home and raise our three children.

Solution

I've got one question for you . . . "Can we trade places?" I've been hoping for my wife to earn a million-dollar income so I can play golf every day, work out, and watch ESPN, but that's just my pipe dream.

As long as you and your wife are on the same page, you're good to go. Before you make a drastic decision, have a serious talk about how this could impact your relationship. If you're really ready to be Mr. Mom, then it doesn't matter what I think. There are some questions you and your wife will need to answer: *Will this change the way you feel about yourself? Will you feel like less of a man since you aren't providing for your family financially? Can you handle what the fellas think? Will your wife treat you differently?*

In Scripture and in society, the husband is generally viewed as the provider, while the wife is the caretaker of the home and family. I know plenty of men who are very good with their children (I'm one of them!), but most often, women are far better at *raising* children. There's no denying that times have changed, but Scripture doesn't give an alternative model for the family other than the father working and the mother being focused on the home. I don't think it's wrong for a wife to work while the husband stays at home, but I do believe that children need the nurturing and special care that only a mother can bring.

Challenge

How do I choose between obeying God and submitting to my husband? I believe that tithing is right, but my husband (who is not committed to the Lord) says we need to use the money for ourselves instead of giving it to the church.

Solution

This is a tough question to answer, so I'll have to go straight to the Word on this one. First Peter 3:1 says, "In the same way, you wives, be submissive to your own husbands so that even if any of them are disobedient to the word, they may be won without a word by the behavior of their wives." Here's the deal: *Even if your husband does not know the Lord, you must still respect and obey his authority.* As a matter of fact, in order to win an unsaved husband to Christ, God not only *commands* submission, but He *uses* it as a powerful spiritual influence in a home. This does not mean that a Christian wife gives in to any and everything that her husband asks. It does, however, mean that you try to win him over by your godly behavior, not by belaboring the issue.

In a situation like this, I would suggest you do two things: (1) Passionately make love to your husband for hours (or minutes depending on his stamina), then immediately afterward affectionately whisper, "Baby, I really love you. May I continue honoring the Lord with my tithe?" If he's not already snoring, he may say yes! (2) If he's still adamant that you not tithe, accept it and continue to be a loving wife. Commit the situation to prayer and stand on faith that God will soften your husband's heart. Remember, an unsaved (or backsliding) husband will not be converted by a wife's preaching or nagging. Christian wives who preach at their husbands only drive them farther from the Lord.

Challenge

How do I protect my credit after a divorce? Most of our debts and savings were listed jointly.

Solution

Spend some time separating and straightening out credit relationships. Divorce can greatly impact your credit score and credit report. Many people who get divorced don't realize how their credit relationship with their ex-spouse can continue to affect them even after divorce.

Here are some ways to protect your credit:

- *Make sure your name is removed from accounts that you are not responsible for paying.* During a divorce, the husband and wife usually work out a division of debts that receives final approval from the judge. Divorcees often think that they are instantly freed from any debt the court assigned to their ex-spouse. Wrong! If the creditors aren't aware of the split, both parties get dinged when the account goes into arrears.

- *Identify all of the accounts and separate them completely.* This includes mortgages, credit cards, bank loans, debit cards, store charge cards, lines of credit, and overdraft checking.

- *Check your credit report for items that should no longer be there.*

Challenge

What can I do about my baby's daddy who refuses to pay child support? I'm a single mother and could really use the financial support to take care of our child.

Solution

Take that joker to court! He helped make the baby and now he should be a real man, step up and take care of his responsibilities.

In the meantime, make sure that your basic financial needs are handled. A place to live, food, transportation, and utilities come first. If you can't afford to pay for anything else, then your other financial responsibilities will have to wait until you have the money. While you're getting things in order, communicate your situation to the bill collectors. Stay in prayer that God will improve your situation.

TEN COMMANDMENTS FOR ROMANCE AND FINANCE

1. Thou shall discuss money in detail while engaged.

2. Thou shall not hide money from thy spouse.

3. Thou shall pool assets with thy spouse.

4. Thou shall consult thy spouse about financial decisions.

5. Thou shall have the best money manager to handle the daily finances.

6. Thou shall submit to an unbelieving husband.

7. Thou shall respect thy spouse, even if thou art the highest breadwinner.

8. Thou shall not "shack up" to save money.

9. Thou shall not make a major financial decisions without spousal agreement.

10. Thou shall keep Christ at the center of your relationship.

PRAYER

Dear Lord, Your Word says that the footsteps of the righteous are ordered by You. So Lord, I thank You for guiding and leading me into the covenant relationship I have with my spouse. We declare what God has joined together, let no man separate. Lord, it is no accident that we are together and we believe that You have ordained our union since the beginning of time. We take authority over the Evil One right now, in the name of Jesus. We pray for a spirit of unity and agreement in our relationship. Help us to get on the same page financially. We pray that Your Holy Spirit will guide us so that we make good financial decisions. Help us to start communicating properly about money to one another and to respect each other's differences. Help our differences complement rather than cause conflict. Help us to appreciate the gifts and perspective that the other brings to the relationship. Give us the grace to forgive and to trust one another, regardless of what has happened in the past.

Lord, give us wisdom about our finances and help us to work as a team. We want to fulfill the destiny You have for us together. Lord, bless our financial life as we are obedient to Your Word. Father, we ask these things in Your precious holy name. Amen.

CHAPTER SEVEN

SAVING, INVESTING, AND RETIREMENT

THE REAL DEAL ABOUT SAVING, INVESTING, AND RETIREMENT

Work your money. Any person who desires to be a good steward of God's resources should want to see his or her money grow. Unfortunately, many people believe they stand a better chance of getting rich from lotteries or sweepstakes than from savings and investments.

The average person in our country is three weeks away from bankruptcy with significant debt, little to no money saved, and is totally dependent on next week's paycheck to keep the budget afloat. Did you know that 35 percent of adults in our country have no savings at all? A lot of us like to spend money but don't like to save it. And although most of us know how to work for money, few know how to put money to work! It's time to save and invest!

Scripture encourages us to save. "The wise man saves for the future, but the foolish man spends whatever he gets" (Proverbs 21:20 TLB). In Proverbs 30:24–25 the ant is commended for saving for a future need. "Four things on earth are small, yet they are extremely wise: Ants are creatures of little strength, yet they store up their food in the summer" (NIV). Savings is the opposite of debt. By saving we make a provision *for* tomorrow, but with debt we make a presumption *on* tomorrow.

I call saving the "Joseph principle," because saving requires self-denial. Joseph saved during the seven years of plenty in order to survive during the seven years of famine. Saving is the act of denying an expenditure today so that you will have something to spend in the future. One of the major reasons most people are poor savers is that we live in a culture of self-indulgence, not self-denial. When we want something, we want it now!

Before you decide *how* you are going to save and invest, you must first determine *why* you should save and invest. You see, as a Christian, money should never be an *end* but instead a *means to an end*. The Word says, "But remember the LORD your God, for it is he who gives you the ability to produce wealth, and so confirms his covenant, which he swore to your forefathers, as it is today" (Deuteronomy 8:18 NIV). God is not against us acquiring wealth, as long as we have a kingdom purpose.

In Matthew 25:14–30, Jesus tells the story of a man who left money for three of his servants to invest. The master commended the first two servants who had invested wisely and then doubled their money. The third servant, however, buried his money and took no risk. He was scared, so he played it safe. The master condemned him, saying, "How dare you take what does not belong to you and not make more with it. The least you should have done was put it in the bank and make me some interest" (verses 26–27, author's paraphrase).

Did you know there are many Christians who are scared to take legitimate risks? They have never taken the time, talents, and treasures God has given or to them for maximum return. The Lord needs more legitimate risk-takers to build a snowball of wealth that can be used for kingdom purposes and passed from generation to generation. History has proven that investing is one of the best ways to accumulate wealth and, more importantly, to pass it on.

CHALLENGES AND SOLUTIONS

Challenge

Tell me, what's the key to saving money? It seems like no matter how hard I try, I'm not able to save any money. Every time I get a little money put away, something happens and there goes my savings!

Solution

Saving money consistently requires self-denial. It may even require a drastic change in your lifestyle. Bestselling financial author Dave Ramsey uses the best example I've heard when it comes to saving money; it's a little extreme, but it makes a powerful point. If a doctor said your child was dying and could only be saved with a $15,000 operation that your insurance would not cover and that could only be performed nine months from today, could you save $15,000? The answer is yes, of course you could! You would sell things, you would stop any spending that wasn't absolutely necessary, and you would take two extra jobs if you had to. For that short nine-month period, you would become a savings madman (or madwoman). You would virtually give up anything to accomplish that $15,000 goal. Saving would become a priority! I think Ramsey's example proves a valid point—we make sacrifices for the things that are important to us.

One of the challenges with saving money is that nobody is going to make you do it. Nobody is going to beg you to save, save, save. Most of what you'll experience will be advertisers and merchandisers telling you to spend, spend, spend! Proverbs says, "Lazy people should learn a lesson from the way ants live. They have no leader, chief, or ruler, but they store up their food during the summer, getting ready for winter" (6:6–8 GNT). Isn't that amazing? The Bible is saying that lazy people (those of us who don't have the discipline to save) need to learn from ants. Although ants don't have anyone leading them, begging them, and beating them over the head about saving, they do it anyway! They store up food for the summer so they'll have something to eat in the winter. That's what saving money is all about, denying an expenditure today, so you will have something to spend in the future.

The most effective way to save is to pay yourself second because you will pay God first. After you tithe, you need to put your savings on automatic pilot. Automatic payroll deduction can be very helpful to ensure that a portion of your income is saved regularly. Have a goal of saving 10 percent of everything you earn. If you can't do that, then save whatever you can, but save something!

Lastly, in order to save money you must begin to build your lifestyle around your savings, instead of trying to build your savings around your lifestyle. In other words, you may have to deny the purchase of the flat-screen TV, computer, DVD player, or new car for now, in order to save money. It won't always be this way, but to get the ball rolling, you must learn to tell yourself no. Remember this quote, "A man who cannot see the ultimate will always become a slave to the immediate."

Challenge

How much should I save for emergencies? Is there such a thing as too little or too much in a savings account?

Solution

The goal is to have a minimum of three months net living expenses in the bank for emergencies. Four to six months would be even better! For example, let's say that it takes you $2,000 to cover your monthly expenses. That includes your rent or mortgage, utilities, food, clothing, savings, entertainment—everything. All you would do is take that number and multiply it by three ($2,000 x 3 = $6,000). That means you need to have at least $6,000 in your savings account for emergencies. Anything less than three months net living expenses in a savings account is too little. Anything more than six months net living expenses is probably too much, and should be invested (unless you are planning a major purchase in the near future).

Now some people call this a *cash reserves* account, or an *emergency fund* account; I like to call it a *rainy-day* fund, because the Bible says that it rains on the just and the unjust (Matthew 5:45). Every now and then it's going to rain in your life. Something unexpected is going to happen. The car may need to be repaired, you may need new tires, or an appliance may break. Unbudgeted things happen in all of our lives, and many of us are not prepared. One of the primary reasons that people get in so much credit card debt is because they don't have an emergency fund. As a matter of fact, the credit card becomes the emergency fund for a lot of people. You and I know that the little things on a credit card today will eventually make you a slave tomorrow.

Finally, it's always good to have money saved in the event of a job loss. An adequate emergency fund will allow you to continue your lifestyle for at least three months, in case you are abruptly fired or laid off.

Challenge

Is playing the lottery or gambling at casinos wrong for a Christian? I enjoy playing arcade games and trying to win a teddy bear when I go to amusement parks. Technically they could both be considered forms of gambling, but I don't believe there is anything wrong with either one.

Solution

Not all risk-taking (which is what gambling is) is wrong. In my opinion, God is not against all forms of gambling and there are legitimate ways to take risk. Buying a raffle ticket is a risk. Investing in the stock market is a risk (you're gambling that your investments will go up and not down). The biggest issue I have when it comes to gambling is the issue of motives and whether or not it is wise stewardship of God's resources. Let's talk about motives first.

There are many reasons that people gamble. Some people *say* they play the lottery because it's fun; others play because they want to contribute to their state's educational programs (yeah, right) or whatever the lottery people say will happen with the profits. Most people gamble and play the lottery for one reason, and for one reason only—because the government has come up with a way to get rich quick!

The Bible clearly condemns the motivation to get rich quick, "The trustworthy will get a rich reward. But the person who wants to get rich quick will only get into trouble" and "A greedy person tries to get rich quick, but it only leads to poverty" (Proverbs 28:20, 22 NLT).

There is also the issue of wise stewardship when it comes to gambling. I just don't think it is wise to throw away money that God has entrusted to you. Now when I say throw away money, I mean that literally. You have a better chance of striking oil in your backyard or being hit by lightning —twice—than you do of winning the lottery. When you gamble at casinos and play the lottery, the odds are stacked against you. It is almost a guaranteed way to lose money! In my opinion, that's just not good stewardship.

Placing your money in the stock market, on the other hand, is an investment decision and a way of planning for the future. With the help of a financial advisor, your chance of increasing your funds should outweigh the risk.

Challenge

What should I do with the 401(k) retirement plan from my previous job? Am I required to move it now that I have a new job?

Solution

You've got four options with the money in your 401(k), but only three of them are good:

1. *Stay with your old 401(k).* This may make sense if the fund has top-quality investment choices, however, most people don't like to leave their money with an old employer.
2. *Roll over the money into an IRA.* Since you can move a rollover IRA to just about any bank, brokerage fund, or mutual fund family, you have far more investment options than a 401(k) account. Most people take this option, which is what I typically recommend.
3. *Roll over the money into your new 401(k) plan.* If your new employer's plan gives you a good fund lineup and useful services, then there's nothing wrong with taking advantage of it. Rolling over to a new 401(k) plan usually gives you the right to take a loan out against the balance of your new account, which is something you can't do with an IRA or with a 401(k) balance held by a former employer. It's a nice perk, but you shouldn't borrow against your 401(k) unless it is an extreme emergency.
4. *Cash out the money.* This is not a smart thing to do. If you want to have some money when you retire, please resist the urge to cash out. This is not "free" money! If you are under age 59 1/2, you will have to pay federal and state income taxes on the money you take out, plus a 10 percent early withdrawal penalty. This could eat up 40 to 50 percent of what you withdraw.

Challenge

What should be my priority: saving for my retirement, or investing for my children's college education? Money is tight and I don't see how I can do both.

Solution

This is a hard question to answer, so I'm going to answer it from a purely financial standpoint. First of all, let me say that I know you love your children, and you want to help them fulfill their dreams and achieve success. Like most good parents, you want to be able to fund their college education. Similarly, you also want to make sure you can retire comfortably, and you're probably concerned whether or not you'll be able to do that.

A study by Boston College's Center for Retirement Research found that about 40 percent of baby boomers (those born between 1946 and 1964) may not be able to maintain their standard of living in retirement. Time is running out for a lot of people, so they need to save now and save big. Therefore, from a purely financial standpoint, I think your retirement should take priority over funding your child's college education.

Your soon-to-be college student son or daughter has other financial options, but you don't. They can work in order to pay their way through college. It may take them longer to graduate, and it will certainly be more difficult, but in the end they'll earn a degree. They can also apply for financial aid, scholarships, and student loans. There are no scholarships for retired people, or financial aid, or senior citizen loans to help you to get by. Sometimes they don't even have jobs for retired people. My recommendation is for you to make your retirement the priority and look for other ways to put your child through college.

MONEY FACT

Among families, 68 percent have saved nothing—or close to nothing—toward their child's college education.

Challenge

Is there a simple rule of thumb to determine how much I'll need for retirement? I'm diligently saving money, but I have no clue what I'll need for retirement.

Solution

Conventional wisdom is that you'll need 70 to 75 percent of your preretirement income to maintain your standard of living after you stop working. If you now make $50,000 a year, you'll need $35,000–$38,000 in retirement. The scary part is determining how much money you will have to accumulate to generate that type of income, year after year.

If you want $38,000 the first year and plan to increase that amount each year, in line with inflation (assuming you play it safe), you'll need $600,000 to $700,000 in today's dollars. That means you're going to have to save $600,000 to $700,000. Where is that money going to come from? Folks used to depend on a mix of pensions and Social Security to fund their retirement, but now a lot of employers are seeking to freeze or terminate pension plans. At the same time, the continuing debate over Social Security makes those benefits far from certain. That means Americans are increasingly on their own when it comes to creating a stream of reliable income to fund their retirement. The tax-free growth provided by retirement accounts such as IRAs and employer-sponsored 401(k)s can make the task easier.

Challenge

What's the difference between a stock, bond, and a mutual fund? Which one of these investments is best for me?

Solution

In my opinion, unless you are a very sophisticated investor, you should invest in mutual funds. Let's look at the differences among stocks, bonds, and mutual funds to help you determine what's best for you.

A share of *stock* represents ownership in a company. That's why they are sometimes called equity investments. People who invest in stocks believe that they can build wealth by owning a part of a successful business. As that business prospers, so does the investor. By the way, this is how Warren Buffett, a billionaire, made most of his money.

A *bond* is a loan, or an IOU, in which the bond buyer (you) lends money to the bond issuer (a corporation, government, or municipality). Just like any loan you make, the bond issuer pays interest to the bond buyer until all the money has been repaid (which is called the maturity date). Because bonds offer a steady stream of interest income, they are called fixed-income securities.

A *mutual fund* is a collection of stocks, bonds, or money-market securities that is owned by many investors and managed by a professional investment company. When you invest in a mutual fund, your dollars are pooled with other investors' dollars. The fund's management team uses that money to build and manage a portfolio of securities. Each fund has an investment objective or strategy that dictates, in general, which securities are bought for the fund's portfolio.

The advantages of a mutual fund are: (1) *professional money management*—expert portfolio managers study the markets to make informed decisions on your behalf, (2) *diversification*—you are not dependent on one type of security or company in your portfolio, (3) *variety of investment choices*—you can choose a fund based on your financial objective, (4) *low minimum investment*—many fund minimums are as low as fifty dollars, and (5) *liquidity*—you can sell your shares at their current net asset value, anytime.

Challenge

Is the stock market a good place to invest?

Solution

I think the stock market is an excellent place to invest, if you have a long-term time horizon. Over the long term, there are not many investments that have done as well as the stock market. To prove my point, below are the results from stocks, bonds, bills, and inflation from 1925–2004, according to Ibbotson Associates:

- Small-company stocks: .....12.7 percent annualized return
- Large-company stocks: .....10.4 percent annualized return
- Government bonds: ....5.4 percent annualized return
- Treasury bills: ....3.7 percent annualized return
- Inflation: ....3.0 percent annualized return

Challenge

If I want to invest money, where should I start? I just received a sizable inheritance from my grandparents and after I pay off some bills, I'll still have a large sum of money left to invest.

Solution

For someone who has never invested before, I strongly recommend that you find a good financial adviser. As a matter of fact, I think even experienced investors need a financial advisor. Great actors and entertainers have coaches, as do great athletes, so why not maximize your wealth-building potential with the assistance of a financial coach? If you don't know anyone, you can get recommendations from trusted friends and family members. Interview a couple of people, then choose the one with whom you feel most comfortable. Whomever you choose, make sure they have the following characteristics:

- *Experience* (preferably at least three years or more in the business)

- *Integrity.* They all say they have integrity, but not all of them do.

- *Expertise.* Does their investment philosophy work? Talk to their other clients.

- *A good teacher.* He/she must be able to make complicated matters simple and easy to understand.

- *Shared values.* Are your values about life compatible?

Those are just some of the qualities you can look for in a good financial advisor. You also need to pay attention to warning signs. Beware of an advisor who:

- tries to rush you into making an investment decision

- offers an unusually high profit or interest rate that is "practically guaranteed"

- talks investment jargon instead of plain English

- goes overboard to impress you (with their car, house, etc.)

- is vague about fees and how he/she is compensated

- does not adequately explain the potential risk of an investment

Lastly, educate yourself about investing. Visit Web sites like www.fool.com, www.msn.com and www.yahoo.com. These Web sites contain excellent information about investing, especially for a beginner.

Challenge

What's the difference between a Roth IRA and a traditional IRA? Is one better than the other?

Solution

Deciding whether to open a Roth IRA or traditional IRA is a major decision with potentially large financial consequences.

Both forms of the investment retirement account are great ways to save for retirement, although each offers different advantages.

With a standard IRA you can deduct the amount you put into the account from your current taxable income each year. Once you retire, you will pay income tax on the money you withdraw from the account.

With a Roth IRA, it works the opposite way. You don't get a current tax deduction, but when you take withdrawals in retirement, there are no taxes owed. Remember, the standard IRA *defers* taxes on the growth and income generated within the account until you start taking out funds. The Roth IRA *eliminates* these taxes. Retirement withdrawals from a Roth IRA are completely tax free. This is why, for most people, the Roth is the better IRA choice.

Let's use a real-life example. If you earn $50,000 a year and put $2,000 in a traditional IRA, you will be able to deduct the contribution from your income taxes (meaning you will only have to pay tax on $48,000 in income to the IRS). At age 59 1/2, you may begin withdrawing funds, but will be forced to pay taxes on all of the capital gains, interest, dividends, etc., that were earned over the past years.

On the other hand, if you earn the same $50,000 income and put the same $2,000 in a Roth IRA, you would pay tax on the full $50,000 income because there is no income tax deduction. If you needed the money in the account, you could withdraw the *principal* at any time (although you will pay penalties if you withdraw any of the *earnings* your money has made). When you reach retirement age, you can withdraw all of the money, 100 percent tax free. The Roth IRA is going to make more sense in most situations. Unfortunately, not everyone qualifies for a Roth. A person filing their taxes as single cannot make over $95,000. Married couples are better off, with a maximum income limit of $150,000 yearly.

Challenge

Should I convert my traditional IRA to a Roth IRA? Does it matter when I make the change?

Solution

You can switch a traditional IRA to a Roth IRA at any time. You'll owe income tax on the money you convert, but in return you can get at your savings tax-free in retirement.

You're eligible if your modified AGI (adjusted gross income) is not above $100,000, although this requirement will be dropped in 2010, opening conversions to everyone. Make the switch if:

- You want to hedge against the possibility that you'll face a higher tax rate in retirement, and . . .
- You can pay the conversion tax with money you have outside the traditional IRA, and . . .
- You want access to tax-free income after you retire, which gives you more flexibility to manage your tax bill.

Challenge

When should I begin investing for my retirement? I'm in my twenties and money is very tight, so I've decided to wait until I'm in my thirties or forties to set up a retirement fund.

Solution

Waiting to invest for retirement is a mistake and could cost you a lot of money in the long run. Always remember, the early bird gets the worm!

Let's look at what happened to two young ladies, both twenty-one years old. Jenny decided that she would buckle down immediately and put $1,000 a year into a Roth IRA, which was great. She also decided to do this for just eight years, from age twenty-one to age twenty-eight. Then she would stop investing and use her income to play from that time on. Her friend Lakisha thought she'd be more serious and take a longer view. She would get her youthful playing out of the way for those same eight years, then beginning at age twenty-nine, she would invest $1,000 a year each year into her Roth IRA all the way to retirement.

Here's how the numbers work out. Jenny invested $8,000 over eight years. Lakisha invested $37,000 over thirty-seven years but didn't begin until eight years after her friend started. We'll assume their investments each averaged a 10 percent annual return.

If you're like Lakisha, you're probably thinking she'll end up with a lot more at retirement, because she invested nearly five times as much as her friend Jenny. At age sixty-five, however, Jenny, who invested only $8,000 over eight years, will see her investment realize *more* growth than Lakisha, who invested every year for thirty-seven years!

Here are the results: Jenny will retire with $427,736 in her Roth IRA; Lakisha will have $363,043. Why did Jenny's $8,000 grow more than Lakisha's $37,000? *Because time magnifies compound interest.* Jenny started earlier, so her money had more time for compound interest to work its magic. That's why the earlier you start, the better! Even $1,000 left alone to earn 6 percent a year will multiple to $39,000 in twenty years! That's the power of compounding. (To see how $1,000 grows over extended periods at several rates of interest, look at "Understanding Compound Interest," page 231.)

Challenge

Is it possible for someone to catch-up if they've never invested for retirement? I'm over fifty years old and I don't have anything saved up for retirement.

Solution

The bottom line is that you need to become a savings madman or madwoman! First, ask yourself, *why haven't I been able to save?* Have you been living above your means; investing money in your children? Is it that you simply never made saving for retirement a priority? Whatever the reason, you need to deal with it, and correct the behavior that caused you not to save.

Secondly, you've got to make some very tough decisions that could involve downsizing your house, driving a cheaper car, or starting a side business. Whatever it takes, you must free up some money and put it away for your future.

The good news is, since you are fifty years old, you can contribute more to retirement accounts than those who are under fifty. These are called catch-up provisions. For instance, in 2007 the maximum contribution for a traditional IRA and Roth IRA is $4,000. For those fifty and older, the max is $5,000. For a 401(k) contribution it's $15,000; however, if you are over fifty it is $20,000. I'm sure as the years go on you'll be able to contribute even more because of these catch-up provisions.

Challenge

Can I withdraw money from my 401(k) for a down payment on a new home, without incurring a penalty? I heard that I won't get hit with a penalty since I'm a first-time home buyer.

Solution

If you haven't owned a home for at least two years, the federal government will allow you to withdraw up to $10,000, penalty free, from your 401(k) to use for a down payment. Although you won't get hit with the 10 percent penalty, you will still have to pay income taxes on the amount you withdraw. If you are in the 30 percent tax bracket, the $10,000 is reduced to $7,000. I'm not saying don't do it, but that money is not free. You still have to pay Uncle Sam.

Challenge

Is it a good move to borrow money from my 401(k) to pay off high-interest credit card debt?

Solution

Borrowing money from your 401(k) is the wrong move to make for paying off credit card debt. I know it sounds like heaven because you've heard all the good things about this strategy: five years to pay it back, a low interest rate, and the fact that you're actually paying the loan interest back to yourself. Hey, if your credit card rate is 18 percent and you can borrow from your 401(k) at 8 percent, it sounds like a good move. Well, not really. Let me give you three reasons why.

First, although you contributed to your 401(k) with pretax dollars (money you have never paid taxes on), when you start to repay the loan, you'll have to repay it with after-tax money (money that has already been taxed). Therefore, you actually pay back more than you take out. When you eventually start withdrawing that money after you retire, it's going to get taxed all over again. You would be paying taxes twice, on the same money! That's not a wise investment. If this isn't enough to deter you, I know the next few points will get your attention:

Second, 401(k) loans are good only as long as you stay with the company. If you decide to leave, or you get fired or laid off, in most companies, the balance of what you owe is due at the time you leave! I know a guy who borrowed from his 401(k) and planned on paying it back in three years. Unfortunately, a few weeks later he got fired and the $5,000 loan was due in full, immediately! They gave him a little extra time, but he still couldn't pay it. After six months went by (and he still hadn't repaid the loan), the company reclassified the $5,000 loan as a 401(k) distribution (believe it or not, that is legal), and the $5,000 became income. The poor guy was taxed and penalized on the

$5,000 "loan" he took out. In other words, what started out as a loan became a taxable distribution, all because he was unexpectedly released from the company.

Third, if you borrow money from your 401(k), you are taking money out of the stock market. If the market is moving up, this could mean lost opportunity. During most robust periods in the stock market, the majority of the annual gains are made in just a few months. In a year where the market is up, say, 10 percent (which is a good annual return), 8 percent of the 10 percent return likely came in two consecutive months. Therefore, if you missed those two months, your annual return would have only been 2 percent for the year! You see, in order to make your money grow, you must stay in the market. (That's why taking it out is a big risk.)

Challenge

Should I keep my 401(k) investments in safe, stable investments, or should I venture back into the stock market? A few years ago, right after the 9-11 terrorist attacks on America, my retirement account lost over half of its value when the stock market went down. I had most of my 401(k) in my company's stock and a few stock mutual funds. It scared me so much that I moved the money to something safe (bond funds) and that's where it has been every since. I am in my late thirties.

Solution

Like a lot of people, your retirement account got clobbered after the September 11, 2001 terrorist attacks. Even people who had rock-solid stock portfolios got hit pretty hard. So don't feel bad just because your portfolio went down. There are some things you could have done to prevent the sharp decline that your portfolio experienced.

First, *never invest more than 10 percent of your company's stock in a 401(k) plan.* Do the names Enron and WorldCom ring a bell?

People who worked for those companies did the same thing you did—they put most or all of their 401(k) assets in the company's stock and now they have nothing. When the company went belly-up, so did their retirement accounts. Limit investment in your company's stock to no more than 10 percent of your portfolio, no matter how much you love the company!

Second, *always diversify your investments.* A few stock mutual funds along with your company's stock may not have been enough to be adequately diversified. When you invest in stock mutual funds, you need at least four different investment styles represented: (1) large-company stocks, (2) medium-company stocks, (3) small-company stocks, and (4) international/global stocks. Even real estate (REITS) should be considered.

Some people think that just because they have one mutual fund, their investments are diversified. That is true, as it relates to one style (large companies for instance), but it isn't true as it relates to the market in general. Believe it or not, not all stock funds, move in tandem. When large-company stocks are doing well, sometimes small-company stocks are languishing and vice versa. Even the Bible says we need to always diversify: "Invest what you have in several different businesses, because you don't know what disasters might happen" (Ecclesiastes 11:2 NCV).

Third, *don't panic. Let time work for you.* When investors pull their money out of stock funds in fear and put them into bond funds, they've panicked; that's not a good long-term move. Instead of selling your stock funds, you should have been trying to find a way to buy more! Every five years or so, the stock market "goes on sale." Rich people see this as their opportunity to "buy low," but regular folks get scared and pull their money out. If those folks who pulled their investments had stuck with the stock funds and let time work for them, their portfolio probably would have made up the decline and even gained some by now.

The stock markets over the past few years have been good, but those who kept their entire portfolio in bonds missed an opportunity to make up what they lost. I'm not saying bond funds are bad, but for those who are nowhere near retirement—whether in your late thirties or even early fifties—having a 401(k) that consists primarily of bond funds will not accomplish their goal of growing their assets over the long haul.

TEN COMMANDMENTS FOR SAVING, INVESTING, AND RETIREMENT

1. Thou shall pay God first and pay yourself second.

2. Thou must build thy lifestyle around savings, instead of thy savings around lifestyle.

3. Thou shall establish a "rainy-day" fund.

4. Thou shall save at least 10 percent of thy income.

5. Thou shall start investing for retirement as soon as possible.

6. Thou shall invest in mutual funds versus individual securities.

7. Thou shall always diversify and let time work to thy benefit.

8. Thou shall not borrow from thy 401(k).

9. Thou shall not panic when investments decrease in value; hold on.

10. Thou shall find a good financial advisor with the heart of a teacher.

PRAYER

Dear Lord, I thank You for all of the resources You have placed under my stewardship and I acknowledge that everything I have belongs to You. Lord, help me to save and invest on a regular basis and not to consume all that I have. Give me the tenacity to say no to things I want today, so I can say yes to things I will need tomorrow. Help me to make the right decisions. Show me how much I need to give, spend, and save. Lead me to the right counselors who will help me stay on track toward my financial goals. Lord, help me to look into the future and make wise choices that would be best for Your kingdom and my family, not only now but in the years to come. Keep greed far from me and help me to exercise caution and patience. Everything I do I will give You honor and praise, in Jesus' name I pray. Amen.

CHAPTER EIGHT

REAL ESTATE AND MORTGAGES

THE REAL DEAL ABOUT REAL ESTATE AND MORTGAGES

There's no place like home. At the conclusion of the classic movie *The Wizard of Oz,* Dorothy realized everything she had experienced was just a dream. The yellow brick road, the Munchkins, and the Wicked Witch of the West were not real. When she woke up from her magnificent dream, she uttered those heartfelt words, "There's no place like home." Dorothy was so right. In the lives of most Americans, there is no place like home. Better yet, there's nothing like owning your own home. Owning a roof over your head and the land under your feet is the great American dream.

When someone buys a home, it usually represents the largest investment and the most serious financial decision that person will ever make in their lives. A home is more than bricks and mortar. It is more than just a financial asset. A home is a place to live and raise children, plan for the future, and create memories. It's also an investment in your community. Home ownership reinforces family stability, responsibility, asset-building, and self-esteem. For most people, home ownership has become a critical factor in moving up the economic ladder.

Most Americans seem to agree. According to the Fannie Mae Corporation:

- A whopping 86 percent of Americans believe they are better off owning than renting.
- People who own their own homes live in communities four times longer than renters.
- Of all consumer spending, 30 percent is for housing and home-related goods.

According to the Department of Housing and Urban Development (HUD), home equity is the largest single source of household wealth for most Americans. Due largely to the appreciation of home property as well as equity buildup, the median net wealth for home owners exceeds $78,400; in contrast, renters accumulate less than $2,300, or 3 percent of this amount. For home owners, almost 60 percent of wealth is in the form of home equity. For minority home owners, home equity is an even more important component of wealth. It represents more than three-fourths of their median net wealth ($48,300), almost one hundred times the median wealth of the average black renter (barely $500). For owners in the lowest income brackets, equity in single-family homes constitutes more than half their wealth, HUD reports.

When you throw in the tax advantages of home ownership, the economic evidence is clear in affirming that home ownership is a good investment that increases wealth for families of all races and incomes. All it takes is perseverance, planning, and preparation and the great American dream can be yours.

CHALLENGES AND SOLUTIONS

Challenge

Should we continue to rent or is it better to buy a home? My wife and I have been renting for five years, but everybody tells me that renting is throwing money down the drain.

Solution

Although home ownership is generally preferable to renting, that does not mean you should automatically try to buy a place. Whenever you are comparing buying to renting, you must look at what you can afford. Because housing is so expensive in some areas of the country, it may be better to continue renting until you can afford to buy a house. If your rent payments are substantially cheaper than what you would pay on a house, then, believe me, you are much better off renting. However, *in most situations, I believe a person is better off buying than renting, if all things are equal.*

Below are some pros and cons of owning and renting.

MONEY FACT
Things being equal, it's usually better to own your home than to rent. You build equity and get to write off your mortgage interest.

BUYING ADVANTAGES

- You build equity, and therefore build wealth.

- The property appreciates over time, increasing its value and contributing to your net wealth.

- Interest paid on home loans is tax deductible.

- You feel a sense of community and stability.

- You are free to customize decor and landscaping to suit your style and needs.

BUYING CONSIDERATIONS

• You're responsible for maintenance.

• You pay property taxes.

• There is a risk of foreclosure and loss of equity.

• A family has less mobility; it's harder to move than as a renter.

RENTING ADVANTAGES

• A renter has little or no responsibility for maintenance.

• Short-term contracts make it easier to move.

RENTING CONSIDERATIONS

• There's no income-tax benefit.

• There's no equity.

• There's no control over rent increases.

• You risk eviction; the landlord is owner and makes the decisions.

Remember, it is better to buy only if it fits your budget. You'll see more on this topic in the budgeting section.

Challenge

I'm a home owner, but I'm behind on my mortgage payments; what can I do? Because of some unexpected financial adversity, I can no longer afford to make my mortgage payments on time, and to make matters worse, my adjustable rate mortgage (ARM) went up.

Solution

According to *USA Today*, almost 5 million American families are expected to see their adjustable rate mortgages reset to higher rates this year and next. For borrowers who started with low teaser rates, the higher payments may be too much to bear, especially if they have other financial pressures.

Since you've fallen behind on your payments, here are a couple of things you may want to do.

First, contact your lender. Inform the bank as soon as you know your payment will be late. If the payments are already late, go ahead and call the bank. Banks adopt a very different attitude if they know the facts and know that the owner is not trying to skip out on the loan. But if you dodge them and won't take their calls, the bank will definitely adopt a hard-core attitude.

In a lot of instances, people are afraid to call the bank because they don't believe their lender will help them, and some are even afraid the lender will use any information against them to foreclose faster. There is a huge myth out there that financial institutions want to take the property back. They don't want the house, they want their money, so most of the time, they'll work with you. Foreclosing on a home, then reselling it costs a lender almost $59,000, on average, according to Freddie Mac.

Second, when you contact your lender, offer the bank or financial company some options. See if they'll agree to:

- Refinance your current loan. You could refinance from an ARM into a fixed rate loan.

- Repayment plan. Long-term "catch-up" plans allow home owners to gradually bring their loan up-to-date by paying more per-month on the mortgage.

- Loan modification/restructure. Change the interest rate or other terms of the loan.

- Forbearance. Postpone the interest or payments on the loan for a fixed period of time.

- Quick sale. Arrange to sell the property for less than the loan and the bank may consider the loan paid in full.

Challenge

What is better, a fixed rate or an adjustable rate mortgage loan?

Solution

I recommend that when interest rates are historically low (which they are at this writing) home buyers should get a fixed rate loan instead of an ARM. If you currently have an adjustable rate mortgage, convert it to a fixed one as soon as possible. As you probably already know, an ARM is adjustable and can go up or down. Most people get hurt when they base what they can afford on the minimum payment of the ARM, not taking into account that ARMs can move upward (which means a higher monthly payment).

The only time an ARM might be worth the risk is if the fixed rate mortgage is about 2 percent higher than the ARM and the ARM can increase by only a maximum of 2.5 percent. Then the most you would have to risk is one-half of 1 percent.

However, many people who get ARMs don't have those kinds of caps, and some of these mortgages can go up 4, 5, even 6 percent or more. This is a ticking time bomb, waiting to explode! Remember the biblical warning: "Sensible people will see trouble coming and avoid it, but an unthinking person will walk right into it and regret it later" (Proverbs 27:12 GNT).

Challenge

What's the deal with interest-only loans? I've found the house of my dreams, but I'm not sure I can afford the mortgage payments. My mortgage broker recommended an interest-only loan, but I don't know how they work or what the risks are.

Solution

Your dream house may turn into a nightmare if you finance it with an interest-only loan. They are very dangerous and I don't like them. Let me tell you how these loans work. You (the borrower) take out a mortgage loan, but you only pay interest on the loan for a period of three, five, seven, or ten years. During that time your mortgage payments are lower, which is very tempting. At the end of that period, the mortgage payment is increased to include both the principal and interest portions of the loan. The new payment amount is typically higher because now there is less time to pay off the loan's full amortized amount. In other words, you have only twenty to twenty-five years to pay off the mortgage, instead of the standard thirty.

The main reason most people use these loans is it allows them to get more house than they can actually afford. These loans allow people to "fake it." People get lured by the initial lower payments, which makes them think they can afford the house. Others use interest-only loans because they are only planning to stay in the house a short time. Some use the loans because their income varies each month and they figure they make enough money to pay on the principal. Still others say they do it to free up cash so they can make other investments.

If you already have an interest-only loan, I recommend two things: (1) refinance into a traditional loan, or (2) pay extra toward the principal before the interest-only period ends, in order to offset the increase in the payment.

Challenge

How much can my wife and I afford to pay on a monthly mortgage? We've been prequalified for a mortgage and aren't absolutely sure we can afford the monthly payment.

Solution

In my opinion, your house payments should be no more than 35 percent of your net spendable income (that's income minus taxes and tithes). That means if you bring home $3,000, then the most you should spend on your monthly house note is $1,050. By the way, most financial professionals will warn you not to buy a house with a price more than two times your current salary. Let me warn you, though, just because a mortgage lender tells you that you can afford a certain amount, that doesn't mean you actually can. You also have to take into account your giving, saving, and other lifestyle choices. The lender doesn't take those things into consideration; you have to figure that out for yourself.

One of the biggest mistakes I see is when young married couples qualify for a mortgage based on both of their incomes. They get the largest house and the maximum mortgage loan they can "afford." After a few years (or a few months), they have children and decide the wife should become a stay-at-home mom. There's only one problem—she can't. The couple can't afford for her to quit because they've based their mortgage (and lifestyle) on both incomes. The number one financial problem facing most young couples is they spend too much on housing.

Challenge

Is it better to pay off my mortgage or to keep taking the tax deduction? I just received an inheritance (Praise the Lord!) and it's enough money for me to pay off my mortgage, but my friends tell me that would be stupid because I'll lose my mortgage tax deduction. They also told me that paying off my home is not a "good investment." They suggested that instead of paying off the mortgage I should invest the money in stock mutual funds or somewhere else to get a better return.

> **MONEY FACT**
> The word *mortgage* comes from the root words *mort* (death) and *gage* (grip), so "mortgage" means "death grip."

Solution

Don't listen to your friends. They don't understand risk. If you have the ability to pay off your

162

mortgage, by all means do it! That being said, let's deal with the tax deduction issue first. Now stay with me on this, because most people don't really understand how this whole thing works.

As a home owner you do get a small tax break for paying mortgage interest, but it only serves to slightly reduce your effective mortgage interest rate. For every dollar you pay in mortgage interest, your income taxes are reduced by that portion of a dollar equal to your tax bracket. In other words, if you're in the 28 percent tax bracket, each dollar of mortgage interest you pay reduces your income taxes by 28 cents. So you're paying a dollar to get 28 cents back. Does that sound like a good deal to you? No, it's not! If you pay a dollar in mortgage interest, then get 28 cents back, you are still out 72 cents. Therefore, you didn't make money by paying interest, you lost money.

Now suppose you didn't have a mortgage. Your friends are right; you would not have the tax deduction. Therefore, the dollar that would have been going to pay mortgage interest is now taxed by the government at 28 cents (assuming you're in the 28 percent tax bracket). The truth is, you'll be way ahead to pay off your mortgage and give the government their 28 cents in taxes on each income dollar. You get to keep the remaining 72 cents because you won't be sending that dollar to the mortgage company as interest, and the last time I checked, 72 cents was worth more than 28 cents! In essence, your friends are telling you to send a dollar in interest to the bank so you won't have to send 28 cents in taxes to the IRS. That's crazy! If you think that's a good deal, then mail me $10,000 and I promise I'll send you back $2,800 as soon as your check clears!

Don't get sucked into this flawed logic. I would rather live debt free and not make a dollar trade for a return of 28 cents. Go ahead and pay off your house as fast as you can!

Lastly, let's deal with whether investing in a good growth stock mutual fund (or another high-return investment) is better than paying off your home mortgage. The reasoning your friends followed is very common. They are basically saying that if you can average 10 percent on your stock mutual funds (some years it may be better, some years worse, but the long-term average for large-company stocks is about 10 percent) and you pay a 6 percent mortgage rate, you get to keep the 4 percent profit on the spread. A lot of businesses operate this way and make plenty of money. They borrow money at a lower rate and invest the cash in something that pays them a higher rate. They make their profit on the spread. There are two reasons why this is *not* a good deal for most home owners: *risk* and *taxes*.

This is a risky deal because there is no guarantee you'll make 10 percent on your mutual fund investments. Secondly, investing in mutual funds is not as safe as paying off your mortgage. Paying off a mortgage has no risk. If I own my home, but you have a mortgage, then who's taking the most risk? You are. If I lose my job or get sick, I don't have to worry about losing my home. If you have a mortgage and something happens to you, they could take your house. Debt always causes risk to increase. Let me say it another way . . . investing your windfall instead of paying your mortgage is like taking equity out of your home and investing it in the stock market. You probably wouldn't do it because of the risk involved when investing in mutual funds (there are no mutual funds that can guarantee a return). You have to account for risk when you are making any investment comparison, failing to do so is not prudent.

You also have to account for taxes. If you made 10 percent or 15 percent on an investment, you would still have to pay taxes on your gains, which would lower your profit on the spread. For a 10 percent investment return, the after-tax profit may only be 8 to 8.5 percent.

The bottom line is that after adjusting for taxes and risk, you don't come out that much ahead by investing your money in lieu of paying off your mortgage. You may not come out ahead at all. So the financial advantage (if there is one) is minimal at best, but the advantage to your peace of mind (because you have a paid-off mortgage) is huge! I'll take peace of mind, over a few extra dollars any day!

Challenge

What's the best way to pay off our mortgage early? Should we just take out a regular thirty-year mortgage and pay extra on it, or should we sacrifice and get a fifteen-year mortgage?

Solution

There are a few ways to pay off a mortgage early, but I believe the best way is to force yourself to do so. Therefore, a fifteen-year mortgage is best. Let me tell you why I say that. Most of us have good intentions when it comes to paying off our mortgage early. We take out a thirty-year loan and swear to God that we'll make extra payments toward the principal every month. Our intentions are good, but the road to mortgage slavery is paved with good intentions. Most people just don't do it. The FDIC says that 97.3 percent of people don't systematically pay extra on their mortgage. Odds are you probably won't, either.

It's not because you don't want to, it's just that sometimes life happens; the kids need braces, clothes, and money for school activities. We tell ourselves we'll pay extra on our mortgage, but we just don't do it. We lie to ourselves. So in order to keep you from lying and deceiving yourself, just take out a fifteen-year mortgage, if you can. I know it's going to be tough and a little bit tight, but if you make some lifestyle adjustments, you can do it. Yes, you'll be paying more per month, but you'll also save tens of thousands, if not hundreds of thousands of dollars. A fifteen-year mortgage *forces* you to pay it off in fifteen years and is the only way to guarantee you'll do it.

If you just aren't brave enough to do a fifteen-year mortgage, then pretend that your thirty-year mortgage is a fifteen-year mortgage. Simply make the payments as if you had a fifteen-year mortgage and your house will be paid for in fifteen years. That way, you're not locked in, but you can still accomplish the goal. In addition, you'll save yourself literally thousands of dollars in interest payments.

The least painful way to pay your mortgage off earlier than thirty years is to make additional monthly prepayments; it doesn't matter what the amount is. For instance, make your regular payments, then write a second check made payable to "principal only." Mortgage loans are simple-interest loans, meaning that the interest is calculated on the unpaid balance at the beginning of the month therefore, you have prepayment privileges. Also, the more principal you pay down, the less interest you pay on the next payment. The advantage of prepaying using this method is that there are no up-front fees and you determine the amount of the payment based on available funds.

Challenge

What do you think about biweekly mortgage loans? My lender wants to charge me $500 to set up a biweekly mortgage refinancing deal, which he says will allow me to pay the home off faster and save thousands of dollars in interest costs.

Solution

It's a great idea to retire your mortgage loan as soon as possible. A biweekly mortgage basically allows you to make one extra month's payment per year. If you have a $1,000 monthly mortgage, you would pay $500 every two weeks, rather than $1,000 monthly. There are twenty-six weeks in a year (on a biweekly basis), so you pay thirteen payments rather than twelve. That means you would end up paying $13,000 a year if you paid it biweekly

($500 x 26 weeks). If you paid the mortgage the regular way, you would pay $12,000 a year ($1,000 x 12 months). That's why you pay off the mortgage faster; you're paying $1,000 more each year!

However, *avoid biweekly mortgages that require an up-front cost (like $500) for the service.* In that case, you can create your own free biweekly plan by simply making an extra partial payment per month. All you need to do is send in one extra mortgage payment per year and tell the lender to apply all of the payment to the loan principal, not the interest. If you don't want to do it that way, then just take your regular monthly payment and divide them by twelve. Then add that sum to your regular monthly payment. For instance, if your monthly payment is $1,000, divide it by twelve and you get $83. When you send in your regular mortgage payment, write a second check, marked "payable to principal only," in the amount of $83 and you will, in fact, make one extra payment per year. Doing this will accomplish the same thing without incurring the up-front cost.

Challenge

Is it better to put a large down payment on a home or a small amount?

Solution

Put down enough to comfortably afford the monthly payments. The amount you put down on a mortgage really depends upon your personal financial situation. Some people can put a lot down and still not be "cash poor." Others shouldn't put a lot down because it would deplete most or all of their cash reserves. The ultimate goal is to be able to put down at least 20 percent, so you can avoid paying private mortgage insurance (PMI).

You want to avoid the extra charge of PMI, which is basically foreclosure insurance. If you do not have at least 20 percent down when you purchase the home, the lender requires you to purchase insurance to make sure they get paid, in case you flake out. This is an added monthly charge, typically about $70 per each $100,000 borrowed. You can get rid of this PMI if you pay the 20 percent up front. You can also cancel your PMI insurance if your home goes up in value enough to cover it. For example, if you have a $200,000 mortgage on a house valued at $220,000; that means you have $20,000 of equity (or 10 percent). You would have to continue to pay PMI. However, suppose your home increased in value to $250,000. Now you have a $200,000 mortgage on a house valued at $250,000, therefore your equity would be $50,000 (or 20 percent) and this would be enough equity for you to drop your PMI coverage.

PMI typically comes out of your pocket, as a separate cost from the mortgage. One option that many people use is to roll the PMI cost into the mortgage. Yes, it will boost the cost of your mortgage, but you are essentially paying off the PMI over thirty years, so PMI becomes part of your payments, which are tax-deductible. PMI usually adds 1 percent to your mortgage cost per year. If you're financing a $150,000 home, you'll pay an additional $1,500, so your new mortgage total would be $151,500. Your monthly mortgage will be a little higher, but remember; it's tax deductible, paying PMI separately is not.

Challenge

What should I know before buying rental property as an investment? I hear all of these real estate gurus on TV talking about how easy it is to get rich investing in real estate. Is it really that easy? I feel like I'm missing out.

Solution

Investing in rental property has become increasingly popular in recent years. That's not surprising if you consider the potential rewards—you can generate rental income and also profit from increasing housing prices. Every time I channel surf, I see somebody's real estate infomercial on television. Everybody and their grandmother seem to have the secret to getting rich in real estate! Don't believe the hype. It is never as easy as they make it seem on TV. Most of these people are salespeople who make more money selling their seminars, books, and "get-rich-quick" systems than they do following their own advice. I'm not saying that they are all bad, but you'd better be careful and do your homework. Success as a landlord requires more than collecting rent checks and riding the real estate market. There's real work involved and substantial risk.

If you're thinking seriously about buying rental property, here are some tips that can help you make an informed investment decision:

- *Make sure your financial house is in order.* If you are going to play the real estate game, you'd better make sure you can afford it. No matter what they tell you about the "no money down" deals, you still need to be financially healthy to succeed as a real estate investor. You need to have some money saved, little or no consumer debt, and you especially need to have good credit. Getting into real estate is not something "broke" people ought to consider.

- *Make sure you crunch the numbers.* Unlike a primary residence, rental property isn't an emotionally driven purchase, it's an investment. As an investor you should think about it primarily in terms of profit and loss-risk and reward. Whether you come out on top will depend mostly on two factors: cash flow and appreciation. Consider how much rent you can collect each month and how much will be left over after mortgage payments, maintenance costs, and other expenses. That's your cash flow. In terms of appreciation, know that as a rental-property owner you can't rely solely on appreciation to make your investments profitable, but it can certainly help.

- *Know your market.* The key ingredient to any successful real estate transaction is location, location, location! It pays to know something about the market conditions in the area before you take a plunge. If apartments are in short supply, you probably won't have trouble filling yours. When you are trying to generate positive cash flow from a rental property, vacancies are perhaps your greatest enemy. They cost you money and generate no income in return. Your first line of defense against vacancies is a good evaluation of the rental market before investing. Talk to Realtors and property managers in the area and check the frequency of rental listings in the local paper. Keep in mind that certain neighborhoods, such as those near schools or universities, may have higher demand for rentals than others.

• *Prepare for the commitment.* Owning a rental property is more than an investment; it's a business. You have to be willing and able to commit the time and resources necessary to run your business successfully. Whether you are actively involved in the day-to-day operations or hire someone to manage them for you, make sure you understand how much time and money you will have to spend before you invest.

TEN COMMANDMENTS FOR REAL ESTATE AND MORTGAGES

1. Thou shall build equity by owning instead of renting a home.

2. Thou shall be proactive and contact thy mortgage lender if you fall behind on payments.

3. Thou shall not use an interest-only loan.

4. Thou shall convert an adjustable rate mortgage (ARM) into a traditional loan.

5. Thou shall pay no more than 35 percent of thy net spendable income (that's income after taxes and tithe) on a monthly mortgage payment.

6. Thou shall strive to pay off thy mortgage as soon as possible.

7. Thou shall not take equity out of thy home to make a risky investment.

8. Thou shall pay on a thirty-year mortgage as if it is a fifteen-year mortgage.

9. Thou shall make a large enough down payment so that thy monthly mortgage payment is comfortable.

10. Thou shall diligently prepare before investing in rental property.

PRAYER

Dear Father, I believe that the earth is the Lord's and all it contains—the world, and those who dwell in it. Therefore, I pray that You will give me wisdom and insight regarding real estate and mortgage issues. Help me to find the right home, buy it the right way, and pay it off as soon as possible. Lord, I acknowledge that Your ways are higher than man's ways, so help me to keep my eyes on You and not what everybody else is doing. Bless my home and may it bring glory and honor to You. Guide me in any financial decision I have to make regarding a place to live. I pray this in Jesus' name. Amen.

CHAPTER NINE

LIFE INSURANCE AND ESTATE PLANNING

THE REAL DEAL ABOUT LIFE INSURANCE AND ESTATE PLANNING

A rolling stone leaves nothing behind. I was with my mom the first time I heard The Temptations' hit single, "Papa Was a Rolling Stone," with its sad refrain, ". . . and when he died, all he left us was alone." Even as a little boy, this song by the famous Motown singing group taught me about the importance of life insurance and estate planning. When I asked my mother what the song meant, she said, "Son, it's about a man who didn't take care of his family, and then he died, and all he left his family was alone—no life insurance, no estate plan, no money, no inheritance, no assets, no nothing!"

Unfortunately, when it comes to leaving stuff behind, even men who stay true to their marriage vows die and at times leave their families empty-handed, just like the man The Temptations sang about. Far too many men and women are financially unprepared for the day they "meet their maker" because of procrastination, fear, and ignorance about life insurance and estate planning.

I know talking about life insurance and estate planning isn't very exciting. Neither of them is sexy; they can't be driven like a nice new Porsche; they can't be worn like a sharp suit. In fact, *you* never get to use them! The big payoff doesn't come along until you're gone. Yet estate planning and life insurance are still two of the most important aspects of financial planning.

The Bible says, "Good people will have wealth to leave to their grandchildren" (Proverbs 13:22 GNT). One of the best ways to ensure that your family is taken care of, for generations, is to have the proper amount of life insurance and to do adequate estate planning.

We tend to shy away from talking about life insurance and estate planning because they make us think about death instead of life. Nobody wants to think about dying, but let me throw a statistic at you: 100 percent of all people born will eventually die. The death rate has never changed. In other words, there is a 100 percent guarantee that you will die sometime.

Another way to look at life insurance and estate planning is to think about the quality of your family's life once you're no longer around to take care of them. If you want to ease the burden on your family and loved ones when you make the "transition," then attend to these four areas: (1) estate planning, (2) a will or living trust, (3) life insurance, and (4) financial records.

Estate planning is not just for the rich. Some of you are probably thinking, "Man I don't have an estate, I'm broke!" Well, if you own more than the clothes on your back, you've got enough to put in a will or living trust! If you died today, I bet somebody you know will be fighting over your car, stereo, and even that sweater you wore yesterday! Everything you own, including your debt, is going to be someone's inheritance or responsibility once you stop breathing.

The Bible teaches that we bring nothing into this world and will take nothing when we die (1 Timothy 6:7). Estate planning teaches us that even though we can't take it with us, we can at least determine who gets to keep it. Estate planning essentially decides who gets your property after you die. It also dictates the wisest legal transfer method(s) for leaving your property to those people.

Remember the saying, "Where there's a will, there's a way"? Well, it's true. And without a will the way is unknown and the government often steps in to give *their* way. *You need a will* (or its cousin, the living trust). Amazingly, almost seven out of ten Americans die without wills, but only 20 percent of African-Americans have a will. A well-constructed will is essential, unless you want the state—the government or the "man," whichever you prefer—to carve up your assets. (You might not have much, but I know you don't want the government all up in your business.) A will can spare your parents, spouse, and children the nightmare of delays, family battles, and escalating attorneys' fees that often go into settling a will-less estate.

Don't skimp on life insurance. The most important asset you own is your ability to earn an income. Since you don't know whether you're going to die tomorrow, fifty years from now, or somewhere in between, life insurance provides a source of income for your family, no matter when your last day on earth arrives.

Organize your financial records now. Part of estate planning is organizing your legal and financial records so the right people, like your spouse, trusted family member, executor, trustee, lawyer, and/or planner can easily find them. It makes sense to keep one copy of a document with your estate attorney or planner and one copy at home in a fireproof file. Don't put wills, living trusts, or powers of attorney in a safe-deposit box since these are often sealed at death. If critical information is stored on your computer, make a disc copy and a paper copy.

Begin to communicate with your family about the details of your insurance, will, and overall estate planning. Face the reality of your mortality, and don't let the fear of dying paralyze you. Start planning *now*!

CHALLENGES AND SOLUTIONS

Challenge
How do I know if I need life insurance?

Solution
It depends on who you are. Let's start with the folks who generally *don't* need life insurance:

- Single parents with no dependents.

- Working couples without kids and for whom the premature death of one partner will not affect the survivor's ability to cover the daily cost of living. Note: A small policy can defray funeral costs.

- Retirees who no longer have financial obligations, such as a mortgage or college expenses.

- Wealthy people who already have an estate large enough to provide for a spouse's lifestyle.

- Children. Unless a child's income supports parents, guardians, etc., (as may be the case with a child actor), there's generally little reason for them to have life insurance. However, buying insurance on a child can provide another benefit: guaranteed insurability later in life. This is relevant in the event a child develops an illness, such as diabetes, that makes obtaining insurance nearly impossible or at best extremely expensive. If you have insurance in place prior to the onset of an illness, the policy remains in force and can often be extended, though the cost will increase.

You *need* life insurance under these conditions:

- *You have dependent children.* The loss of your income could affect your spouse's ability to remain in the family home with the kids or to provide the level of care or education otherwise afforded on your salary.

- *You're married to a nonworking spouse.* Your death will likely affect your spouse's ability to pay for food, rent, etc., since going to work for the first time or after a long hiatus could mean a lower-paying job and a diminished standard of living.

- *You have a working spouse whose income is substantially less than yours.* You should consider life insurance because your higher income affords a lifestyle your spouse couldn't afford alone.

- *You have special-needs siblings or others you support or wish to care for.*

- *You are married and/or have dependents and still have a large mortgage remaining on the home.* A life insurance payout will help a spouse pay off or pay down the balance, easing the burden after your death.

In some cases life insurance can serve as an estate planning tool, but that's generally for people with large multimillion-dollar estates. The above points are based on using life insurance to replace a lost income.

Challenge

Should I buy mortgage insurance? My wife and I just bought a new home a few months ago and have been bombarded by offers to buy mortgage insurance. It sounds like a good idea since it offers to pay off the mortgage if one of us dies.

Solution

Even though a mortgage insurance policy sounds like a good idea, I say don't buy it. Yes, a policy would provide great coverage, but mortgage insurance is essentially a high-priced term-life policy. Instead, if you want funds to repay the mortgage, factor that into your needs with a standard life insurance policy.

Challenge

How do I determine how much life insurance I need? I'm not sure if I should take out another policy.

Solution

There's no one-size-fits-all solution because the greater your financial need, the more life insurance coverage you require. Most people need enough life insurance to cover five to ten times their annual salary. For this example, let's say you require seven times your average salary. If you bring home $50,000 a year, your life insurance need would be $350,000. This method is pretty simplistic because it doesn't require you to address any specific insurance needs you might have such as the cost of your children's college education. Whatever the case, $350,000 may not be enough or it could be too much.

The method I prefer to use is based on a person's financial needs and is the most detailed approach to assessing life insurance requirements. It involves determining the expenses you need to cover and how much those expenses are going to cost years or decades from now. If you decide to use this method, there are five primary areas you must evaluate:

1. *Funeral expenses.* Dying is not cheap; even a plain, wooden box (if you can find one) and an unmarked grave will cost several bucks. When you purchase an insurance policy, you can determine the amount of coverage applied to funeral expenses so your family won't have to pass the collection plate on the way to the cemetery.
2. *Your family's lifestyle.* Life insurance can replace the income your family will lose after you die. Without it, your wife and kids may have to sell the house, the cars, and the furniture, and move in with your mother. (I don't know about your mother, but mine ain't havin' it!)
3. *The children's education.* Without the benefits of life insurance, your children may not be able to afford a higher education once you enter the Pearly Gates. Wouldn't it be awful to gaze down from heaven and see your child flipping burgers instead of wearing a cap and gown?
4. *To pay off any outstanding debts.* Don't make your family

grieve twice—first about your death and then about the debt you left them. If planned properly, insurance can pay off the mortgage, car note, credit card, and more.

5. *To pay estate taxes.* Did you know that your heirs could actually get taxed on the assets you leave them? According to 2006 tax laws, leaving more than $2 million in assets (including insurance proceeds) could force your heirs to pay estate taxes.

With this method you should also evaluate the liquid assets you currently have in place. If you have already saved for much of your child's college education costs, for example, there is little reason to include that in your insurance coverage.

MONEY FACT

Almost one out of four women is broke within two months of a husband passing away.

Challenge

What's the difference between term- and whole-life (or cash-value) insurance, and which one should I get?

Solution

Let me explain the difference between the two before I tell you which one is better. Term-life insurance is in place for a specific term, typically ten to thirty years. It is purely death coverage. There is no savings component, and the premiums increase with your age. It's also cheap. If you have term-life insurance, you are basically renting coverage.

With cash-value or whole-life insurance, part of your premium buys a death benefit, and part funds a savings component with a small interest rate. It's similar to buying a home (versus renting) because you can accumulate cash account value or equity in the policy. Unlike term insurance, the policy doesn't expire after a set period of time. As long as you pay the premiums, the policy remains in effect. But because of the dual structure (death benefit and savings), cash-value premiums are typically four to eight times more expensive than a similarly sized term policy.

For most people, the best approach is to buy term insurance and invest the additional premiums they'd otherwise pay for a cash-value policy into something else. I'm not saying that cash-value life insurance is bad, but most people I know are underinsured. If stuck with only cash-value insurance, they wouldn't be able to afford enough insurance to adequately cover them (because it costs more than term). Sometimes a combination of term and cash value works well (with term being the bigger policy). Whichever you choose, you have to consider cost, coverage, and complexity (meaning you better understand how it works).

Challenge

Is it wise to have all my life insurance through my employer? The policy I have seems to be adequate.

Solution

No, it is not wise to have all of your life insurance through your employer. Some of it, yes, but definitely not all of it! There are a couple of reasons why it's not a good idea:

1. *You may leave or get fired from your job.* If that happens, you'll lose benefits, including insurance coverage. I knew a guy who had all of his life insurance through his employer. He got laid off and was out of work for about five weeks. Then, without warning, he had a heart attack and died! Now that's jacked-up. Not only did the family lose a loved one, they lost the life insurance benefit because he was unemployed and never purchased additional coverage above what his former employer offered.

2. *You also want to have an additional policy to protect your insurability.* If you develop an illness, such as cancer, finding affordable insurance, or any at all, will be difficult. If you have insurance in place outside of your employer, prior to the onset of an illness, that policy remains in force and can often be extended, though the cost will increase.

Challenge

Should I cash in a cash-value life insurance policy to catch up on my bills? I am experiencing some serious financial problems because I got laid off and my policy has some equity in it.

Solution

Cashing in your insurance policy is an option, but it may not be the best way for you to solve the problem. If you cash in the policy, you can take the cash value out and use it to pay your bills, but then you'll be left without insurance (remember what happened to the guy in the previous example). That's a big chance to take, unless you know exactly when you're going to die.

You can also borrow the cash value and pay it back. (The life insurance company uses your policy as collateral.) The best part is that unlike other loans, you can't be declined. Still, interest is due, and if it's not paid, it will be tacked on to the loan. Eventually, you'll have to repay the loan with interest or risk the policy lapsing (leaving you without insurance).

A third option is to borrow money from the policy and *don't* pay it back. If you do this, your outstanding loan reduces the death benefit of your insurance by the amount of the loan, plus interest. If you allow this to go on long enough, you could eventually consume the entire value of your life insurance.

The most important thing is to make sure that you are living within your means. I know some people who borrowed against insurance policies, and paid off debt, only to find themselves right back in debt because they never dealt with their spending habits.

Challenge

Do I need disability insurance? They offer it through my job, but I don't really understand what it's for.

Solution

Everybody needs disability insurance. Out of all the different kinds of insurance, disability is the most overlooked. Disability insurance is essentially paycheck protection. If you're sick or injured and can't work, disability insurance replaces up to 70 percent of your income. It allows you to pay most or all of your bills. Just because you're injured, the bills won't stop coming and with disability insurance neither will the money.

If you're under thirty-five, statistics say there is a 65 percent chance that, at some point in your life, you'll experience a disability that will keep you out of work for at least six months and possibly as long as two years. (If you think the creditors are on your back for being two months late, try two years.) Furthermore, 48 percent of all mortgage foreclosures occur because the home owner did not have disability insurance coverage.

Some employers offer short-term and long-term disability plans. If your employer offers it, sign up ASAP, even if the heaviest thing you lift at work is a pencil! (Disability insurance is not just for people with physical or risky jobs.) The policies employers offer are usually cheaper than any policy you could get on your own. Keep in mind that, just like life insurance through your job, this benefit disappears when you leave, and it cannot be converted to an individual plan. When you change companies, please don't procrastinate about getting a new disability policy.

Challenge

What is long-term care insurance and when is the best time to consider one? I'm forty years old and have been told I need to get it now.

Solution

Long-term care insurance (LTC; notice, this almost looks like TLC) covers any chronic or disabling condition that requires long-term nursing care or constant supervision. Long-term care refers to care in a nursing home, nursing care in your own home, and help with the activities of daily living, such as dressing, eating, bathing, and taking medicine.

Statistics show that at least 6.4 million people aged sixty-five or older need long-term care and that one out of two people over the age of eighty-five require care. At least half of the population who are eighty-five or older will need help with daily living activities. Such care is provided when someone can no longer independently carry out essential, everyday activities like eating, bathing, dressing, etc. Most people think of long-term care as something needed by older people, but an accident or illness can strike someone of any age. When it does, they too may find themselves in need of assistance.

In my opinion, the right time to get LTC insurance is around age sixty. Some agents will encourage you to buy it when you turn forty, because as you grow older premiums increase and your chances of passing underwriting screens decrease. In reality, you will likely have more pressing financial commitments in your forties and fifties (retirement or a child's college education) than you will at sixty. Premium prices don't really spike until after age sixty anyway. So unless your family history gives you reason to think your health could fail at a young age (a parent with early onset Alzheimer's, for example), you should probably wait.

Challenge

I hear that everyone needs a will, but what exactly is a will and why do I really need one? With our second child on the way, my wife and I are even more concerned about protecting our kids.

Solution

A will is a document that establishes who should receive your stuff. It protects the people you care about and makes sure they get what you want them to have after your death. Without a will, the court makes these decisions.

In brief, there are three primary reasons you need a will:

1. To determine who will inherit your assets. The person receiving the inheritance is called a *beneficiary*.
2. To determine who will manage your estate. This person is called an *executor*.
3. To determine who inherits the kids (this person is called the *guardian*), if they're still minors, or if they have special needs that will continue into adulthood.

Challenge

I hate to think about stuff like this, but suppose I am in a serious accident and don't die but become incapacitated, who makes the decisions for me? Is there something I can do now that will protect me if this happens?

Solution

If this happens, you'll become totally reliant on someone else (giving the term "my brother's keeper" new meaning). Make sure you have these three things in place: (1) a *durable power of attorney*, (2) a *health-care proxy*, and (3) a *living will* (different from a regular will).

Here's an abbreviated description of each:

- The *durable power of attorney* assigns someone to handle your finances if you become incapacitated.

- A *health-care proxy* assigns someone to make medical decisions for you.

- A *living will* states whether you want extraordinary means (life support or resuscitation) used to prolong your life when you're critically ill.

Challenge

What's the difference between living trusts and wills? Which do you recommend?

Solution

Both documents allow for the transfer of property when you die. With a will, you name the property (or identify it in some way) and the beneficiaries who receive the property. Almost all wills have to go through probate, a court approval process, which is time-consuming and expensive and, in almost all cases, provides no benefit except to the lawyers involved. A will is the traditional document that's been used for many centuries.

A living trust is the alternative transfer method that does not require probate. It allows you to transfer all, or at least most, of your property to beneficiaries after you die, without the expensive courts and lawyers getting involved. The bottom line is that a will goes through probate, and a living trust does not.

TEN COMMANDMENTS FOR LIFE INSURANCE AND ESTATE PLANNING

1. Thou shall realize that estate planning is not just for the rich.

2. Thou shall create a will.

3. Thou shall make sure adequate life insurance coverage is obtained.

4. Thou shall organize thy financial records.

5. Thou shall not buy mortgage insurance.

6. Thou shall not buy cash-value life insurance, unless thou can afford to do so. (For most people, term insurance will do.)

7. Thou shall never have all of thy insurance coverage through thy employer.

8. Thou shall purchase disability insurance.

9. Thou shall go beyond a basic will and implement a durable power of attorney, health-care proxy, and a living will.

10. Thou shall use a living trust instead of a basic will to transfer thy property to beneficiaries.

PRAYER

Dear Lord, help me to deal with the reality of my own mortality. Help me to stop procrastinating about a will, life insurance, and estate planning. Lead me to the right advisors and give us wisdom as we plan. Lord, I cast down any thoughts or imaginations that are not from You. Give me and my family the freedom to discuss these difficult issues and help me to make the right decisions. In Jesus' name I pray. Amen.

CHAPTER TEN

YOUNG ADULTS AND CHILDREN

THE REAL DEAL ABOUT YOUNG ADULTS AND CHILDREN

Young, restless, and broke! For young adults (twenty-something), being broke is a very likely possibility! Nearly two-thirds of young people are experiencing some type of financial pressure: struggling with late payments, chronic bounced checks, little to no savings, bad credit, and heavy student loan debt.

The current generation of young people has sometimes been called Generation Broke, but it's not all their fault. Young adults have had to endure the most aggressively marketed society in the history of the world! More advertising impressions fly in front of them in one month than my generation saw between 1977 and 1979!

Everywhere you look it's about the bling-bling, especially in rap videos where even twenty-year-olds have tricked-out Escalades, designer clothes, and gorgeous women. These images make it *look* like entertainers have more money than Donald Trump, so how can you blame today's youth for wanting to live the same way! To top that off, the most aggressively marketed product in our culture is debt! With five billion credit card offers in our mailboxes in 2006 alone, the message is that easy payments are a way of life. No wonder it's so hard to get ahead financially when you're young. The pull of the culture and materialistic values make it difficult to get and stay financially healthy.

Another reason why young adults encounter financial trouble is that no one's teaching them the proper ways to handle money. Schools don't teach money management skills and most parents avoid the subject altogether.

The good news for young adults is that they've got something their parents and grandparents don't have or at least they've got more of it—time. No matter how many mistakes they make, if today's youth can get on the right track now, they have the time to turn their financial life around and set themselves up for a great financial future.

There are three strategies that a young adult can use to transform their finances.

First, know your credit score. If there is one single thing that will have the biggest impact on turning a young person's finances around, it would be the FICO score. Just about every financial move they make for the rest of their lives will be somehow linked to the FICO score.

A FICO score is a three-digit number that determines the interest rate to be paid on credit cards, car loans, and home mortgages. (For more information, review pages 60–61.) It can also determine one's ability to get a cell phone or have an application for a rental apartment accepted. It affects auto insurance premiums and the ability to get a job! That's right, most employers will pull a credit history before making a hiring decision!

Young adults should also make sure bills are paid on time, and keep overall debt load at reasonable levels. The goal is to get and keep one's credit score above 700. Remember, "A good name is to be more desired than great riches" (Proverbs 22:1). From a financial standpoint, a credit score determines whether or not an individual has a "good name."

Second, strategically pay off student loan debt. For those who feel like college loan debt is a heavy weight to carry, be assured, it was a great investment! Over the course of an individual's working life, a bachelor's degree is estimated to translate into $2.1 million in lifetime earnings, compared to $1.2 million in lifetime earnings for those with only a high school degree. Collecting a master's degree bumps it up to $2.5 million. The key is paying off the loan. Here are a few tips:

- Work with the lender to find a repayment plan that fits your current financial situation. Remember, extending a repayment period increases the total interest cost over the life of the loan.

- Those with low-rate loans shouldn't rush to pay them off. It may make sense to put any extra money toward paying off credit card debt or saving for a down payment on a home.

- Young adults with loans from a variety of lenders can shop around at banks, credit unions, and other loan sources, such as Sallie Mae (the Student Loan Marketing Association), to consolidate them.

Third, develop multiple streams of income. The days of depending on one stream of income are over! The twenty-something generation is encouraged to find careers they love, but they shouldn't be afraid to diversify from core competencies to earn extra money. It's dangerous, financially, to think that corporate America will always take care of you. Even if you have a good job with a good paycheck, it's still wise to develop multiple income streams. Begin now to develop and diversify sources of income. Don't sit idly on ideas you may have. Nurture those God-given talents and turn them into money-making ventures. You never know when one of those streams will be needed. Ecclesiastes 11:2 says, "Divide your portion to seven, or even to eight, for you do not know what misfortune may occur on the earth."

These are just a few things that young people can do if they want to be young, and wealthy! If you're in your twenties, remember, now is the time to take control of your financial life. Create the financial future you want by doing what it takes today.

CHALLENGES AND SOLUTIONS

Challenge

Do I need a college degree in order to be financially successful? I am undecided on whether or not I should attend college.

Solution

Although I am a college graduate and a huge advocate of a college education, I know that a diploma is not everyone's ticket to a successful financial life. A college degree does not guarantee financial success. I know people who have more degrees than a thermometer and are still broke!

In most cases, however, a college degree (or advanced degree) does help you earn more money. A few years ago the census bureau calculated how different degrees can impact a person's lifetime earnings potential. I've already discussed how earning a bachelor's or master's degree can impact your income, but it doesn't stop there. A professional degree (M.D., law degree, etc.) bumps your potential lifetime earnings to $4.4 million. A degree could very well cause you to earn more money, but what you ultimately earn will depend on your specific career path and how well you perform in a chosen profession.

Earning money doesn't make you financially successful; *keeping* money does. You can make a lot of money, but if you spend it all, you will never build significant wealth.

In my opinion, there are a few other reasons why you should consider pursuing a college education:

- A degree in your chosen field can open up career opportunities.

- Many employers use a college degree as a hiring criterion.

- College is a chance to make new friends and establish lifelong associations.

- College can enhance your knowledge and personal growth.

There are many more reasons a college degree is good, but again, it's certainly not an absolute necessity.

Challenge

I don't have a credit history, so what's the best way to establish credit? I just turned twenty and want to establish credit for myself without going into debt.

Solution

There are four things you can do, two of which I would definitely *not* recommend:

1. *Establish a secured credit card.* This is highly recommended. A secured credit card looks, feels, and smells like a regular credit card but is much safer. Here's how it works: you deposit money with the credit card company, which establishes your credit limit for that card. It's like a checking account; you cannot charge more than you have in the account (that's why they call it "secured"). As long as you're able to make that security deposit, you should be able to get a card. The goal is to use the card responsibly, pay on time, and don't go over the limit. If you do this for about a year, you will have established a track record at the credit bureaus. You can shop for secured cards at www.bankrate.com and www.cardweb.com or at your local bank or credit union.

2. *Piggyback off your parents' credit card.* I also recommend this strategy. Your parents can add you to their credit card account, as an authorized user. If your name is on the account you can start to build a file at the credit bureaus that reflects your parents' credit history. There is one caveat here—your parents need to have a good credit history! If your parents' credit is "jacked-up," then don't choose this option!

3. *Open credit card accounts.* I would not recommend this strategy at all. It's too dangerous and most young people can't handle credit cards because the temptation to spend money is too great and the ability to pay it off is too low. According to *Money Magazine*, the average credit card balance among college seniors is $2,864. The last thing you need to do is to get in over your head with credit card debt.

4. *Open retail store accounts.* I would not recommend this strategy either. Retail store accounts will cause you to shop more and spend more.

Challenge

I am behind on my student loan payments because I lost my job. I just can't afford the payments anymore; what should I do?

Solution

Ask your student loan lender about a deferment or forbearance. Although they are often seen as the same, the two are completely different. A deferment is a temporary postponement of a borrower's student loan repayment. A borrower is entitled to defer his or her student loan payments if the borrower meets certain eligibility criteria, such as unemployment or a temporary disability. Your lender can tell you which conditions qualify for deferment.

In most cases, the government pays the interest on your loan so the balance does not increase during the deferred period.

With forbearance, your lender grants you—at its discretion— permission to reduce or stop your loan payment for a period of time. Interest continues to accrue on your loan, and you'll still have to pay off both the accrued interest and the loan when you resume your payments. Although a deferment is preferable, forbearance is often easier to get because it's not governed by the type of your loan or the date you obtained it. Other options do exist, so contact the lender as soon as possible. Don't let the loan go into default.

Challenge

Where should I place my priorities for a spending plan now that I just started my first job since graduating from college? Should I pay off my student loans and credit cards first or invest in my employer's 401(k) plan?

Solution

It's more important that you knock out the credit card debt first, as it probably has a higher interest rate. Also, the more you can pay off, the better your credit score will be. However, if your employer offers a match on your 401k contributions, that's free money and you can't pass that up. Therefore, as you begin to pay down your debt, go ahead and contribute enough in your 401(k) to get the company match. Once you reach the contribution limit, you can use the remaining money to help pay down your student loan debt.

Challenge

Should we save money for our children's college education even though we're deeply in credit card debt? My kids are young, and I feel bad that we're not putting anything away for them.

Solution

I recommend that you pay off the credit card debt before you build a college fund for the kids. I know you feel like you should be doing more, but you have to deal with reality, and right now you can't afford to get rid of your debt and save for the kids' college education. Getting out of debt is just like making an investment because you are eliminating interest payments. If you invest in your children's education without paying off the debt, you're still not getting ahead. If you are out of debt when the kids are ready to go to college, you will have money freed up from your income that you can put toward their college expenses.

Challenge

What's the best investment for college, a 529 plan or U.S. savings bonds? I need to start saving money for my child's college education, but I'm not sure where to put the money.

Solution

Both U.S. savings bonds and 529 plans can be excellent savings vehicles for many families. Determining which one is the best investment will depend on future market conditions, interest rates, and whether you are willing to take more risk for a potentially higher return.

U.S. savings bonds are backed by the U.S. government and pay a fixed rate. There are two types of savings bonds that most people use for college: Series EE and Series I (also known as I Bonds). Bonds are very safe, but your money-making potential is limited. If a child is older, and just a few years from college, then I think savings bonds are an excellent way to save for college. For younger children I would definitely recommend a 529 plan. They aren't backed by the U.S. government but are invested in mutual funds. Depending on the type of mutual funds chosen and market conditions, a 529 plan may earn more money than savings bonds (but also present greater risk).

Overall, I still like 529 plans better, and here are some of the main reasons:

- Your investments grow tax-deferred, and distributions to pay for college come out federally tax free (and may even stay tax free depending on the state you live in).

- You, the donor, stay in control of the account. You are the one who calls the shots, deciding when withdrawals are taken and for what purpose.

- It's an easy, hands-off way to invest for college. Plan assets are professionally managed (in mutual funds) so you don't have to worry about the day-to-day management of your investments.

- Everyone is eligible to take advantage of a 529 plan, and the amounts you can put in are substantial (over $300,000 per beneficiary in many state plans). Generally, there are no income limitations or age restrictions. If you're thinking about going back to college or graduate school in the future, go ahead and set up a plan for yourself!

Challenge

How can I teach my children about money? They treat me and their father like we're walking ATMs.

Solution

There is nothing wrong with a child asking their parents for money, but that doesn't really teach the child anything about the value of money. It is parents, not MTV or BET, that should be responsible for training children about finances. In general most parents spend eighteen to twenty-two years trying to prepare each of their children for adulthood, but almost no time is spent teaching them the value and use of money. We are to "train up a child in the way he should go, [and] even when he is old he will not depart from it" (Proverbs 22:6).

MONEY FACT

Teens are the number one target for credit card companies.

In order to teach God's principles of finance and money management, I recommend using these three methods:

1. *Talk to your children about money.* Go beyond "How much do you need?" Don't stop at "How much did it cost?" Parents should discuss everything about money, including their own financial successes and challenges. If God blesses you financially, let the children know how it happened. On the other hand, if you're having financial problems, don't completely hide them from your children. Use whatever situation you are in as a teaching opportunity for your children. "These words, which I am commanding you today, shall be on your heart. You shall teach them diligently to your sons and shall talk of them when you sit in your house and when you walk by the way and when you lie down and when you rise up" (Deuteronomy 6:6–7).

2. *Practice what you preach.* Parents must also "practice what they preach" by being good examples. Because children are so impressionable, they easily recognize and adopt their parents' attitudes toward money. Therefore, parents must be godly role models on how to handle money. "Everyone, after he has been fully trained, will be like his teacher" (Luke 6:40). In other words, parents can verbally teach what they believe, but children will imitate their parents' behavior.

3. *Let them practice handling money.* Children need to be given opportunities to see how God's financial principles are applied in the lives of their parents and should be given the chance to apply them. Allowing children to make some financial decisions on their own (with their own money) helps them to experience the consequences of their choices. Will they make mistakes? Absolutely; we all do, but the lessons learned will be unforgettable.

Challenge

What are some practical ways to teach my children how to save, spend, and give? I talk to them all the time about money, but they need a way to put some of the principles into practice.

Solution

Teach your children how to budget when they start receiving an income, i.e., allowance, money earned from chores, etc. Begin with a simple system consisting of three boxes or jars, each labeled separately—*Share, Save,* and *Spend.* The child distributes a portion of his income into each box, establishing a simple and visible budget system. Even a six-year-old can understand this method because when there is no money to spend, the box is empty!

As the child matures, he should also participate in the family budget. It will help him understand the limitations of income and how to stretch money to meet needs. In their teen years, children should begin a written budget.

During the budget training, teach your child to become a wise consumer. Teach shopping skills, the ability to distinguish needs from wants, and the importance of waiting on the Lord to provide.

Challenge

Should I give my kids an allowance? I want to teach my children about money, but my husband doesn't think we should pay them.

Solution

I don't have a problem with paying allowances, but I do have a problem with how most of them are administered. An allowance alone doesn't promote good behavior with money. You can't just put cash in a child's hands and expect him to know how to manage it. Rather than just providing a weekly handout, talk to your kids about what you expect them to pay for (candy, movies, video games) and what they hope to buy (short-term and long-term expenditures). Then help your kids prioritize their goals. Once you set the rules, don't be a pushover by bailing them out if they run out of money five days before the next allowance payment.

TEN COMMANDMENTS FOR YOUNG ADULTS AND CHILDREN

1. Thou shall realize that a college degree doesn't necessarily translate to financial success, although having a degree can be beneficial.

2. Thou shall focus on keeping money that is earned in order to build wealth.

3. Thou shall not build thy credit history by using credit cards and retail store cards.

4. Thou shall build credit history by piggybacking on thy parents' good credit or by a secured credit card.

5. Thou shall ask for a deferment when unable to pay student loans, rather than going into default.

6. Thou shall always contribute enough in your 401(k) to get the company match, even if you are in debt.

7. Thou shall pay off credit card debt before saving for a child's college education.

8. Thou shall teach thy children the value of money.

9. Thou shall teach thy children how to share, save, and spend.

10. Thou shall give thy children an allowance, only when it is accompanied by specific goals and expectations.

PRAYER

Dear Lord, I pray that You will help me to model financial faithfulness to my children. Give me the wisdom to train them in the way they should go so when they get old they will not depart from it. Protect them from bad debt and credit decisions. I pray that they will learn how to deny themselves for the good of their future. I pray that they will never forget the good things that they have been taught. Protect them and give them wisdom. Help them not to become slaves to debt. For my children, I pray this in Jesus' name. Amen.

CHAPTER ELEVEN

BUSINESS AND WORK

THE REAL DEAL ABOUT BUSINESS AND WORK

Butcher, baker, candlestick maker. There's a story often told about the job attitudes of three bricklayers. When asked "What are you doing?" the first bricklayer replied, "Laying brick." The second answered, "Making $9.30 an hour." The third bricklayer proclaimed, "Me, I'm building the world's greatest cathedral." That's the statement of a person with a positive attitude and a godly approach to work.

A job is not merely a task designed to earn money; it's also intended to produce godly character in the life of the worker.

While the bricklayer is building a house, the house is also building the bricklayer; his skill, diligence, and judgment are refined, making him better prepared for God's work.

Productivity is the name of the game in God's kingdom, and the way out of poverty and into financial health is through work. Just as we can't expect to generate wealth by sitting on our butts all day, we also won't increase wealth by approaching work with the wrong attitude. Even before the fall, the time in which sin entered the human race, God started work. "The Lord God took the man and put him into the garden of Eden to cultivate it and keep it" (Genesis 2:15). So the very first thing the Lord did with the perfect man, Adam, in the perfect environment, Eden, was to give him a perfect job. Adam's first charge was to be productive!

There's nothing wrong with being a bricklayer, candlestick maker, or a business owner. According to Scripture, there is dignity in all types of work. God does not elevate one honest profession above another. A wide variety of jobs are represented in the Bible; the Lord Jesus was a carpenter, David was a shepherd and a king, Luke was a doctor, and Lydia was a retailer who sold purple fabric. God is more concerned about the attitude with which you approach your job, career, or business—*how* you do what you do rather than whether you're a geologist or a janitor. If God can use Amos a fig-picker, He can certainly use you in your current position. In God's economy there is equal dignity in the labor of all honest and sincere men and women.

CHALLENGES AND SOLUTIONS

Challenge

I hate my job and want to change careers; what should I do?

Solution

A career change is a natural life progression; most studies show that the average person will change careers *(not jobs)* several times over the course of his or her lifetime. First you need to pray. Then take some time and make sure that you really want to change careers. What you may need is a job change; the same career but a different employer. (A lot of people get frustrated because they don't like their boss or their company, but that doesn't mean they need to switch careers.) There are a few things you can do to make the right decision:

- Discover your true passion; in others words, what would you do for free if money was not an issue?

- Research new careers.

- Talk to your close friends and loved ones.

- Enlist a mentor in the field you are considering.

- Obtain additional training or education.

- Start networking.

Challenge

How will I know when the time is right to quit my job and devote 100 percent of my time to a business I currently operate on a part-time basis? The folks at work are really getting on my nerves and I'm ready to walk out! Besides it'll give me a chance to be a stay-at-home mom.

MONEY FACT

No work is insignificant. If a man is called a street sweeper, he should sweep streets even as Michelangelo painted, or Beethoven composed music, or Shakespeare wrote poetry.
—DR. MARTIN LUTHER KING JR.

Solution

Hold on, sister! Before you leap, make sure you've got a parachute. You will know that you're ready to quit your 9 to 5 job when you accomplish two things:

1. *Have at least four to six months of net living expenses in the bank.* You'll need at least this amount in case the first few months on your own don't produce any income. Instead of spending the money your business venture generates, put some or all of it into a savings account during those start-up months.

2. *Grow the business income to at least match your current full-time income.* This is a signal that if you devoted full-time effort to your part-job, you could make significantly more money.

Challenge

What should I do to prepare for starting a business of my own? I've been in the corporate world my entire career, and I feel like I'm ready to do my own thing.

Solution

There is no exact answer or secret formula for preparing to start your own business. It's different for each individual and type of business, but I strongly recommend doing these three things:

1. *Develop a detailed business plan.* As a result of completing the plan, you will be much better prepared to start and grow the business. In the process of developing a business plan, you'll also discover if your business idea is a feasible one. The plan will also prompt you to answer critical questions like:

   • How is your business unique?

   • Why will your goods or services appeal to customers?

   • What are the primary differences between your company and your competitor's business?

   • Why would customers choose your business over one that offers similar products or services?

2. *Make sure you have adequate capital.* Where will you get the money to start your business? No matter what people say, you do need start-up capital. As I said before, you need personal and business cash reserves. Most businesses fail, not because of lack of knowledge but lack of capital.

3. *Make sure you are suited for business ownership.* Just because you don't get along with your boss doesn't mean you should become a boss. A lot of people who get into business aren't

really cut out for business ownership. Here are a few questions to ask before embarking on a new business career:

- Are you a self-starter?
- Are you a risk-taker?
- Are you willing to work long hours? (Forget about quitting at 5 o'clock every day.)
- Can you make sound decisions? (Have you heard the saying that common sense isn't that common?)
- Do you possess good organizational skills?
- Can you deal with a fluctuating income?
- Are you resilient? (You're going to have to come up with new and creative ways to find new customers, beat the competition, and get things done on a tight budget.)
- Do you have a healthy self-esteem? (It takes a tough skin to deal with the rejection and let-downs that often accompany entrepreneurship.)
- Do you handle money well? (If your personal checking account is constantly overdrawn, your business account probably will be too.)
- Can you attract a diverse customer base?
- How will the business affect your family?

As you can see, a lot needs to be considered before going into business; it takes more than just a great idea. Starting and managing a business takes time, motivation, desire, and talent. It also requires research and planning. Check out what Jesus said in Luke 14:28–30 about the importance of planning: "But don't begin until you count the cost. For who would begin construction of a building without first getting estimates and then checking to see if there is enough money to pay the bills? Otherwise, you might complete only the foundation before running out of funds. And then how everyone would laugh at you! They would say, 'There's the person who started that building and ran out of money before it was finished!'" (NLT).

Challenge

Should I go into debt to start a business? I'd like to go into business for myself, but I don't have the cash to get started.

Solution

The best way to start a new enterprise is with cash; however, as I said concerning debt in chapter 5, business debt is considered "acceptable" debt. There's nothing wrong with borrowing money to start a business.

Although the majority of businesses are started with loans, it is still a very dangerous way to get a new business off the ground because most new businesses fail within the first twenty-four months of operation. If a business doesn't work, the debts incurred still have to be paid.

The number one reason businesses fail is lack of capital. If you decide to borrow money to start a business, make sure that you have adequate cash reserves to cover your living expenses and to maintain the business. Although many business owners borrow money, they still don't have sufficient capital to sustain the business until it can make a profit. That's why I would only recommend borrowing to start a business if you have adequate cash reserves, for your personal use and for the business.

Secondly, whether you should borrow really depends upon the type of loan you're considering. I know people who've started businesses with traditional bank loans or Small Business Administration (SBA) loans (visit www.sba.gov for more info). Each is good because in order to qualify you need a strong business plan. Banks will assess the business risk and your ability to repay the loan. (They wouldn't give you the loan if they thought your business would fail because that would be a bad investment on their part.)

Others I know have borrowed from their credit cards or taken out home equity loans to finance a new business. As a financial advisor I would not recommend borrowing against your home, unless there is an extremely high probability of success. If the business doesn't work, and you can't find another job right away, you'll be left with a bigger mortgage and no income left to pay it off. (A lot of people lose their homes because of business debt that is tied to their personal assets.)

Challenge

What kinds of retirement plans are available for me as a business owner? I want something that's affordable for me and my two employees.

Solution

The plans I like most for small business owners are the *Simplified Employee Pension Plan* (SEP IRA) and the *Savings Incentive Match Plan for Employees* (SIMPLE IRA).

If you have just a handful of employees and are looking for a plan that is truly low cost and low maintenance, then a SEP IRA is a great consideration. It's funded with tax-deductible employer contributions and requires that you cover all eligible employees. Employee contributions are not allowed. With a SEP there is no "plan document," and you don't need to file annual reports with the IRS. Contributions can vary from year to year, so if you hit a lean spell, you aren't locked in.

The SIMPLE IRA is another good plan. SIMPLE IRAs are good for your employees; they allow employee contributions and they mandate an employer match. The trouble with a SIMPLE IRA is that it won't let you sock away as much for yourself. For 2007, annual contributions are generally limited to $10,500 ($13,000 if you are fifty or older as of December 31, 2007) plus an employer matching contribution (up to 3 percent of your salary). If you have a business with less than ten people, then a SIMPLE IRA is a great way to get started.

MONEY FACT

Find something you love to do and you'll never have to work a day in your life.

—HARVEY MACKAY

Challenge

What's your opinion of network marketing or multilevel marketing? A lot of people claim to be making big bucks (even a few of my relatives) and I don't want to miss the gravy train.

Solution

Multilevel marketing (MLM) is a viable business model and some people (very few actually) have achieved tremendous financial success. The real problem is not MLM itself, but rather how *some* people and companies do business. I like the *concept* of MLM; it's been around for years and I know a few people who are extremely successful. As a matter of fact, my wife has done quite well as a Mary Kay sales director, so I get a chance to see a true professional in action every day! I do have some concerns about this whole MLM craze so let's talk about *the good, the bad, and the ugly* of multilevel marketing.

The Good. The best situation is to find a company you like, a product you believe in, and most importantly, a product you'd be willing to use yourself (even if you were not considering getting into the business). MLMs can provide some great opportunities to (1) start your own business, (2) work from home, and (3) have flexible work hours.

In addition, most MLM companies have a very low cost of entry, with the *potential* for producing exceptional revenue. You will also have the opportunity to learn the skill of "selling," which I believe almost anyone can learn if they are properly trained. While very few people can learn to become a brain surgeon or a professional golfer, selling is a skill that just about anyone can master.

The Bad. Like any business, there are some people, as well as some specific companies, that do not operate with integrity. First of all, a lot of people who get into multilevel marketing do so to "get rich quick." The Bible says "A greedy person tries to get rich quick, but it only leads to poverty" (Proverbs 28:22 NLT). Although many organizations entice new prospects by touting the extravagant incomes of some of their most successful people, in reality, most people who enter multilevel marketing do not make a lot of money. The failure rate is very high and many times people are left with a ton of inventory stacked in the garage or high credit card debt from ordering some of that inventory. (Sometimes failure is due to the company's deceptive practices, and sometimes it's because the individual wasn't prepared to work as an entrepreneur.) Getting into any business to get rich quick will leave you broke. In order to have a successful MLM business, you have to treat it like a real job, not a way to make a quick buck.

Another issue about MLM is whether certain companies are pyramid schemes or legitimate companies. *Legitimate* MLM companies offer a way to sell real goods or services through distributors. These plans usually show that if you sign up to be a distributor, you will receive commissions, not only on your sales (of the company's goods or services) but also on the sales of the people you recruit. Therefore a prerequisite is that the plan is based on *tangible* products and services moving through the network.

Pyramid schemes have a similar structure but a completely different focus. To spot a pyramid scheme, look for companies that pay you based on the number of new members/distributors you recruit and generally *ignore* the marketing and selling of products or services. To circumvent pyramids, the Federal Trade Commission *requires* a minimum of ten *nondistributor* customers per month to be serviced by each distributor after a certain period. Without these customers, it is an illegal pyramid.

The Ugly. The most deplorable aspect of MLMs I've noticed is that many companies and salespeople are starting to use the body of Christ to further their own financial gain. Pastors of large churches routinely get calls from MLM representatives who want access to church members. These companies know that churches are ideal environments for MLM prospecting. Now don't get me wrong, it's OK for businesspeople to generate customers from their own church, especially when it happens as a natural course of business. Converting your church into a "fishing pond" for new customers, on the other hand, is wrong. You don't have to take my word for it, read God's Word. In John 2:13-17, Jesus was outraged that people would see the church community as an opportunity to make a profit. After driving the salesmen and their animals out with a whip and overturning the money tables, Jesus said, "Take these things away; stop making My Father's house a place of business" (John 2:16).

Something is terribly wrong when churchgoers try to exploit and manipulate fellow saints for their own personal financial gain. I can't tell you how many times I've been hounded by people during or right after a church service, when they should be thinking about God instead of plotting how to make a quick buck. I've even had people schedule meetings with me under the guise of needing counseling or discussing ministry, when all they really wanted was to recruit me into their business. Now you and I both know that God don't like ugly and that type of bait and switch definitely ain't cute! Jesus didn't hesitate one second to purge the church of those who saw God's house as a place of profit, so if you plan to enroll in an MLM or any other business venture, be mindful that there is a time and a place for everything. Keep God's house sacred and you will be blessed.

Challenge

Is it OK to go into business with someone who isn't a Christian? A friend of mine has a great business idea, but I'm afraid we're unequally yoked spiritually.

Solution

If Christians were more ethical or honest than non-Christians, this would be an easy question to answer. But in twenty-plus years of doing business, I've discovered that you have to be very careful about going into business with Christians too! Still, the Word warns us about partnering with nonbelievers: "Don't team up with those who are unbelievers. How can righteousness be a partner with wickedness? How can light live with darkness? What harmony can there be between Christ and the Devil? How can a believer be a partner with an unbeliever? And what union can there be between God's temple and idols?" (2 Corinthians 6:14–16 NLT). Opposites may attract, but when it comes to doing God's work, it takes like spirits to forge a productive union.

Old Testament law forbade yoking a donkey and an ox as a work team (Deuteronomy 22:10) because they have two opposite natures and would not work well together. It would be unwise and cruel to bind them to each other. In the same way, according to the apostle Paul, it is wrong for believers to be yoked together with unbelievers. He wasn't telling the Corinthians to avoid all contact with the unsaved (1 Corinthians 5:9–10), but they were to avoid "partnerships," which involve the compromise of Christian standards, practices, or goals.

Christianity and secular values are simply not compatible. Therefore, *in most cases it is not wise to go into business with a nonbeliever, especially if the Christian doesn't have majority ownership in the business.* I have seen a few successful partnerships involving a believer and a nonbeliever; however, the believer was the majority owner and his vote and perspective had more weight than the unbelieving minority partner. However, in most Christian and non-Christian partnerships, Christians end up compromising their standards and missing out on God's best for their business.

Challenge

What do you think about mixing business and family or friends? I would love to build a successful enterprise with several of my family members, but I have some reservations.

Solution

There is absolutely nothing wrong with going into business with a family member or close friend, but you have to be extremely careful (as with any partnership). When going into business with someone we know, the tendency is to let our guard down, assuming that there won't be any problems. As a result, many people forgo adhering to basic business practices and procedures, like establishing contracts.

Anytime you go into business with a friend or family member, you should exercise the same caution (if not more) that you would with someone you didn't know well. Perform the same due diligence and follow the same procedures as you would with anyone else. It's not because you don't trust the friend or relative; it's because you are trying to protect the relationship in the event that something goes wrong. (Too often, when the business falls apart, so does the friendship.) If your potential business partner objects or doesn't understand, take that as a sign that you shouldn't be doing business together.

TEN COMMANDMENTS FOR BUSINESS AND WORK

1. Thou shall realize that there is dignity in thy work, no matter what it is (as long as it's legal and moral).

2. Thou shall implement a retirement plan for thy business. (A SEP or a SIMPLE IRA would be great.)

3. Thou shall be very careful about joining a multilevel marketing organization. (Make sure it's not a pyramid scheme.)

4. Thou shall treat thy multilevel marketing business like a job and not like a hobby.

5. Thou shall not treat thy church and fellow church members as prospects for your MLM business, unless it happens naturally.

6. Thou shall not borrow on thy house to go into a new business—and risk not having a roof over your head.

7. Thou shall have a business plan before going into business.

8. Thou shall start a business only if thou art suited for business ownership and have enough capital to start a business.

9. Thou shall not enter into business partnerships with unbelievers.

10. Thou shall be very careful when doing business with family and friends. (Don't ignore normal business practices.)

PRAYER

Dear Lord, I realize that work is a holy calling, so I commit my plans and my business to You. You have given me the power to make wealth by working in the field that You have chosen for me. I know that You are at work in me, ensuring that my business plans are guided by You and will succeed. Thank You for giving me grace, to continually seek knowledge and skill in my area of expertise. Thank You for Your increasing favor toward me in the area of business as I am obedient to Your Word and calling. In Jesus' name. Amen.

Closing

And Another Thing . . .

I've offered many solutions and eleven sets of commandments to help you when your money is funny. I conclude with ideas to be sure your heart and spirit are right, so God can bless your stewardship of all you have. So here are seven concluding thoughts about money:

1. *Ask God to forgive your financial mistakes.* If you have incurred unnecessary debts, lived beyond your means, and done just about everything "wrong" financially, know this: God will forgive you. "If we confess our sins, He is faithful and righteous to forgive us our sins and to cleanse us from all unrighteousness" (1 John 1:9).

2. *Commit yourself to prayer and fasting about your finances.* Financial problems just don't go away by themselves; first you have to do battle on your knees. "Then the disciples came to Jesus privately and said, 'Why could we not cast

it out?' And He said to them, 'Because of the littleness of your faith; for truly I say to you, "if you have faith the size of a mustard seed, you will say to this mountain, 'Move from here to there,'" and it will move; and nothing will be impossible for you. But this kind does not go out except by prayer and fasting'" (Matthew 17:19–21).

3. *Stop worrying so much about money.* Worry stifles creativity, causes stress, and is the enemy of your peace of mind. Worrying will keep you broke and your financial potential unfulfilled. Instead of worrying, think of ways to make money! Jesus said, "Do not worry then, saying, 'What will we eat?' or 'What will we drink?' or 'What will we wear for clothing?' For the Gentiles eagerly seek all these things; for your heavenly Father knows that you need all these things. But seek first His kingdom and His righteousness, and all these things will be added to you" (Matthew 6:31–33 author paraphrase).

4. *Obey the last thing God told you to do.* Sometimes you have to go back to the future. In other words, the key to your financial future may be predicated on your total obedience to something you were supposed to do a long time ago. Have you been obedient to everything the Lord has told you to do? "Faith by itself, if it is not accompanied by action, is dead" (James 2:17 NIV).

5. *Change the way you speak (and think) about your situation.* Start watching what you say about money and how you think about money. You will become whatever you talk about and think about the most. Stop meditating on what you don't have and start believing on God for what you hope to have! "Truly I say to you, whoever says to this

mountain, 'Be taken up and cast into the sea,' and does not doubt in his heart, but believes that what he says will come to pass, it will be done to him" (Mark 11:23 ESV).

6. *Hang around new people.* Whom you hang around is a prophecy of your future. Now I'm not saying you should dump all your broke friends, but I am saying there ought to be somebody in your life who can stretch your thinking. If you always hang around people who think like you, then you will never grow financially. If you are always the smartest person in your social circles, then something is wrong. The Bible says, "Iron sharpens iron, so one man sharpens another" (Proverbs 27:17). Also consider this: "Bad company corrupts good morals" (1 Corinthians 15:33).

7. *Develop an attitude of gratitude.* Never become resentful for what you don't have. Instead, be grateful for what God has provided already. Yes, I know you have big dreams and goals, and you may be disappointed with where you are financially, but believe me, you are blessed! If you have air in your lungs, clothes on your back, food on your table, and a reliable means of transportation, you are better off financially than 85 percent of the people in the world! True wealth starts on the inside. Financial contentment grows out of an attitude of gratitude. "In everything give thanks; for this is God's will for you in Christ Jesus" (1 Thessalonians 5:18).

By the way, about point 7, some of us have a hard time having a grateful heart. To foster a grateful attitude, memorize and repeat the following: "For I have learned to be satisfied with what I have. I know what it is to be in need and what it is to have more than enough. I have learned this secret, so that anywhere, at any time, I am content, whether I am full or hungry, whether I have too much or too little. I have the strength to face all conditions by the power that Christ gives me" (Philippians 4:11–13 GNT).

One final thought: *Always think BIG!* The Bible says, "For as he thinks in his heart, so is he" (Proverbs 23:7 NKJV). Don't succumb to the poverty mentality. Never stop dreaming big. You may be going through challenging times right now, but it won't always be that way. God wants you to be financially healthy. He wants to bless you so you can be a blessing!

Don't give up. Your best and brightest financial days are still ahead of you!

Helpful Tools

YOUR BUDGET PERCENTAGE GUIDELINES

Category	Percent of Income (after giving and taxes)
Housing	25 – 38%
Food	10 – 15%
Transportation	10 – 15%
Insurance	3 – 7%
Debts	0 – 10%
Entertainment/Recreation	4 – 7%
Clothing	4 – 6%
Savings	5 – 10%
Medical/Dental	4 – 8%
Miscellaneous	4 – 8%
School/Child care	5 – 10%
Investments	0 – 15%

ESTIMATED BUDGET

MONTHLY INCOME   _____

Salary   _____
Interest   _____
Dividends   _____
Other income   _____
LESS
  1. Tithe/giving
  2. Taxes (Fed., state, FICA)   _____
NET SPENDABLE INCOME   _____

MONTHLY LIVING EXPENSES

3. Housing   _____
    Mortgage/Rent   _____
    Insurance   _____
    Property taxes   _____
    Electricity   _____
    Gas   _____
    Water   _____
    Sanitation   _____
    Telephone   _____
    Maintenance   _____
    Cable TV   _____
    Other   _____

4. Food   _____
5. Transportation   _____
    Payments   _____
    Gas & oil   _____
    Insurance   _____
    License/Taxes   _____
    Maint./Replace   _____
    Other

6. Insurance   _____
    Life   _____
    Health   _____
    Other   _____

7. Debts   _____

8. Entertainment/Recreation   _____
   Eating Out   _____
   Babysitters   _____
   Activities/Trips   _____
   Vacation   _____
   Pets   _____
   Other   _____

9. Clothing   _____
10. Savings   _____

11. Medical Expenses   _____
   Doctor   _____
   Dentist   _____
   Prescriptions   _____
   Other   _____

12. Miscellaneous   _____
   Toiletries/Cosmetic   _____
   Beauty/Barber   _____
   Laundry/Cleaning   _____
   Allowances   _____
   Subscriptions   _____
   Gifts (incl. Christmas)   _____
   Cash   _____
   Other   _____

13. Investments   _____

14. School/Child care   _____
   Tuition   _____
   Materials   _____
   Transportation   _____
   Day care   _____

TOTAL LIVING EXPENSES   _____

INCOME VS. LIVING EXPENSES

NET SPENDABLE INCOME   _____
LESS TOTAL LIVING EXPENSE   _____
SURPLUS OR DEFICIT   _____

DEBT LIST

Date: _____

Creditor	Describe What Was Purchased	Monthly Payments	Balance Due	Scheduled Payoff Date	Interest Rate
_____	_____	_____	_____	_____	_____
_____	_____	_____	_____	_____	_____
_____	_____	_____	_____	_____	_____
_____	_____	_____	_____	_____	_____
_____	_____	_____	_____	_____	_____
_____	_____	_____	_____	_____	_____
_____	_____	_____	_____	_____	_____
_____	_____	_____	_____	_____	_____
_____	_____	_____	_____	_____	_____

Totals

AUTO LOANS:

_____	_____	_____	_____	_____	_____
_____	_____	_____	_____	_____	_____
_____	_____	_____	_____	_____	_____

Total Auto Loans

HOME MORTGAGES:

_____	_____	_____	_____	_____	_____
_____	_____	_____	_____	_____	_____

Total Home Mortgages

BUSINESS/INVESTMENT DEBT:

_____	_____	_____	_____	_____	_____
_____	_____	_____	_____	_____	_____
_____	_____	_____	_____	_____	_____
_____	_____	_____	_____	_____	_____
_____	_____	_____	_____	_____	_____

Total Business/Investment Debt

CREDIT AGENCY CONTACT INFORMATION

You can order a *free* credit report from each of the three credit reporting agencies once a year at **www.annualcreditreport.com**. It will not include your credit scores. You can contact each agency at the following addresses and telephone numbers:

EQUIFAX—www.equifax.com
To order your report, call:
1-800-685-1111

To write:
P.O. Box 740241
Atlanta, GA
303-74-0241

To report fraud, call: 800-525-6285

To report by mail:
P.O. Box 74021
Atlanta, GA
303-74-0241

Hearing Impaired: 800-255-0056, ask operator to call 800-685-1111 to request copy of your report.

EXPERIAN—www.experian.com
To order your report, call:
888-397-3742

To write:
P.O. Box 2002
Allen, TX 75013

To report fraud, call: 888-397-3742

To report fraud by mail:
P.O. Box 9530, Allen, TX 75013
Hearing Impaired: 800-972-0322

TRANSUNION—www.transunion.com
To order your report, call:
800-888-4213

To write:
P.O. Box 1000, Chester, PA 19022

To report fraud, call: 800-680-7289

To report fraud by mail:

Fraud Victim Assistance Division,
P.O. Box 6790, Fullerton, CA 92634
Hearing Impaired: 877-553-7803
If you wish to dispute information found on the report, here is key contact information:

EQUIFAX
P.O. Box 740256
Atlanta, GA 30374
800-797-7003
[9:00 a.m.–5:00 p.m. Monday–Friday in your time zone]
www.econsumer.equifax.com/elsc

EXPERIAN
NCAC
P.O. Box 9595
Allen, TX 75013
800-583-4080 [9:00 a.m.–5:00 p.m. Monday–Friday in your time zone]
www.consumer.com/consumerr/index.html

TRANS UNION
P.O. Box 2000
Chester, PA 19022-2000
800-916-8800 [8:30 .m.–4:30 p.m. Monday–Friday in your time zone]
www.transunion.com/investigate

SAMPLE COMPLAINT LETTER TO DISPUTE INFORMATION

Once you review your credit report and identify inaccurate information, contact the recording agency (see previous page) to dispute the information and formally request your record be corrected. Here is a sample letter to use:

January 2, 2008

ABC Credit Bureau
100 Main Street
Anywhere, GA 10000

Re: Complaint Letter to Delete Inaccurate Information

To Whom It May Concern:

I formally request that the following inaccurate items be immediately investigated. They must be removed in order to show my true credit history, as these items should not be on my report. By the provisions of 15 USC section 1681i of the Fair Credit Reporting Act of 1970, I demand that these items be reverified and deleted from my record.

Item No.	Company Name	Account Number	Comments
Item 5	RFK Loan Corp.	231-8907-5443	Payments were made on time.
Item 8	Fast Loans Corp.	8743489371	This is not an account of mine.

Since thirty days from the receipt of this letter is your allotted time under the law to reverify these entries, it should be understood that failure to do so within that thirty-day period constitutes reason to promptly delete the information from my file (FCRA 15 USC s1681i (5) (A).

Also, pursuant to 15 USC s1681i (6) (A) of the Fair Credit Reporting Act, please notify me when the items have been deleted. You may send an updated copy of my credit report to the address below. According to the provisions of 15 USC section 1681j, there should be no charge for this notification. Also, please send me names and addresses of individuals you contacted, so I may follow up.

Sincerely,

John Doe
250 Elm Street
Anywhere, GA 10000
SS# 123-45-6789

UNDERSTANDING COMPOUND INTEREST

Saving and Investing $1,000
At Various Interest Rates

Interest	Year 5	Year 10	Year 20	Year 30	Year 40
6%	$5,975	13,972	38,993	83,802	164,048
8%	6,336	15,645	49,423	122,346	279,781
10%	6,716	17,531	63,003	180,943	486,851
12%	7,115	9,655	80,699	270,293	859,142

Saving and Investing $10,000
At a 12 Percent Return

Yields:

$20,000	in	6 years
40,000	in	12 years
80,000	in	18 years
160,000	in	24 years
320,000	in	30 years
640,000	in	36 years

If you would like to contact Lee Jenkins,
you may do so through his Web site:
www.leejenkins.org

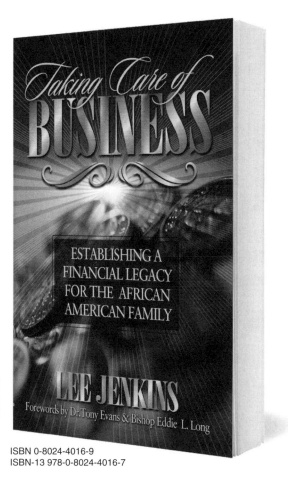

ISBN 0-8024-4016-9
ISBN-13 978-0-8024-4016-7

Lee Jenkins offers readers comprehensive strategies for setting goals in the areas of family, faith, friends, finances and fitness. These goals will transform the hearts and then the lives of people who want to improve their financial situation.

by Lee Jenkins
Find it now at your favorite local or online bookstore.
www.LiftEveryVoiceBooks.com

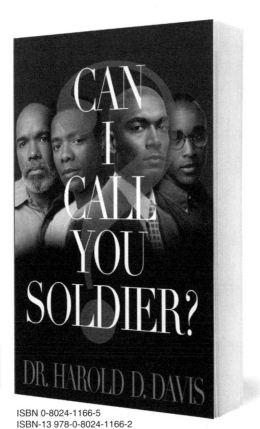

ISBN 0-8024-1166-5
ISBN-13 978-0-8024-1166-2

A generation is under attack…who will protect your family?

The war is at home and the battlefield is in the lives of our young men. In any community, and particularly in the black community, millions of young men feel the void of a role model. For every absent father, complacent leader, and passive bystander, there is someone who will step in and fill the father figure void—whether he is a trustworthy man of God or a dangerous enemy. It's up to us to win this battle and prepare the next generation to join the fight.

"Young men are in desperate need of mentors who model their message. This book challenges the strong among us to become mentors and provides them with the equipment to do so."

   -Rev. William Dwight McKissic, Sr.
   Senior Pastor, Cornerstone Baptist Church

by Dr. Harold D. Davis

Find it now at your favorite local or online bookstore.

www.LiftEveryVoiceBooks.com

ISBN 0-8024-8989-3
ISBN-13 978-0-8024-8989-0

This practical, encouraging and biblically-based manual will help trauma survivors—
and their loved ones—move toward healing. Philadelphia-based, licensed psychologist
Collins describes how trauma victims get caught in the trauma zone, a place they want
to escape but can't. Some can't move forward, feeling stuck and victimized by their past.
Some can't see, living in denial of what has happened. And others can't learn from the
past, repeating the same mistakes over and over. All of them find they can't cope with
the overwhelming emotions that accompany trauma. Dr. Collins believes there is a way
out of the trauma zone and back to emotional health, a path he outlines in this
practical, encouraging book.

by R. Dandridge Collins, Ph.D.
Find it now at your favorite local or online bookstore.

www.LiftEveryVoiceBooks.com

The Negro National Anthem

Lift every voice and sing
Till earth and heaven ring,
Ring with the harmonies of Liberty;
Let our rejoicing rise
High as the listening skies,
Let it resound loud as the rolling sea.
Sing a song full of the faith that the dark past has taught us,
Sing a song full of the hope that the present has brought us,
Facing the rising sun of our new day begun
Let us march on till victory is won.

So begins the Black National Anthem, by James Weldon Johnson in 1900. Lift Every Voice is the name of the joint imprint of The Institute for Black Family Development and Moody Publishers.

Our vision is to advance the cause of Christ through publishing African-American Christians who educate, edify, and disciple Christians in the church community through quality books written for African Americans.

Since 1988, the Institute for Black Family Development, a 501(c)(3) non-profit Christian organization, has been providing training and technical assistance for churches and Chrisitan organizations. The Institute for Black Family Development's goal is to become a premier trainer in leadership development, management and strategic planning for pastors, ministers, volunteers, executives and key staff members of churches and Christian organizations. To learn more about The Institute for Black Family Development write us at:

The Institute for Black Family Development
15151 Faust
Detroit, Michigan 48223

We hope you enjoy this book from Moody Publishers. Our goal is to provide high-quality, thought-provoking books and products that connect truth to your real needs and challenges. For more information on other books and products written and produced from a biblical perspective, go to www.moodypublishers.com or write to:

Moody Publishers/LEV
820 N. LaSalle Boulevard
Chicago, IL 60610
www.moodypublishers.com